Where is There?

SECOND EDITION

Where is THERE?

A SURPRISING JOURNEY
TO HELP YOU FIND HOPE, DIRECTION, AND POWER FOR YOUR LIFE

STEPHEN WALKER

DEDICATION

To Dr. Selwyn McCabe ("Doc") who helped me get THERE, despite myself, and for his friendship and mentoring.

To my two wonderful children, Jeremy and Jessica. The gift of being a father is something I could never have imagined. May your lives continue to grow and expand.

To my amazing, loving wife Rebecca, who is also my best friend! Words can't describe what she means to me, let alone her invaluable help in completing this book.

CONTENTS

Part Three
How Does It Work In Relationships?

PART FOUR
LIFE—THE WAY

Introduction

A lot of people wonder, "What's it all about?" Many search for an answer. Others accept the beliefs of their parents as the way it is. Still others don't consciously think too much about those things. In my case, I was living a comfortable, carefree life at home during college. I had no accountability or job (I vowed never to work) and thought I was *THERE*. That is, until a fateful trip to Africa dramatically changed everything. My surprising story, especially the unusual way it happened, will let you know why I am writing this book.

Between my junior and senior years of college, my flamboyant uncle, a renowned air show headliner, invited me to fly with him to Africa to deliver a rescue mission plane during the Congo revolutions. I thought it would be the adventure of a lifetime. It turned out to be a horror thriller, during which I faced imminent death four times. Add to that, a girl I arranged to go on the trip died. Why did I live? That started a nine-year downhill spiral.

I returned with a lot of inner turmoil and began to make poor decisions. Then came several ongoing illnesses and surgeries.

Things went from bad to worse. It finally got to a point that I felt like someone crawling in a scorched desert, so parched and dry with all hope fading, when a stranger came, tapped the sand, and gave me a drink of the purest and most refreshing water imaginable. Feeling completely different, I instantly knew: *ALL IS WELL!* It was such a surprise that out of my mouth came, "No, no, it can't be that!"

Now what? If this experience was real, it had to work in everyday life. I have included stories of happenings on jobs, in relationships, and in other areas of life that had unexpected surprises and rewards by seeing and responding through a new lens. Each one has jewels and keys that can transform your life, many of which you may not find elsewhere.

New friends got me a fine-dine restaurant job as a server, which I thought was beneath me. But exciting things happened, which was only the beginning. I was very fortunate to meet many wonderful people, including several VIPs, which led to some great personal relationships. An associate once asked me, "How come things happen to you that don't happen to us?" The answers are what this book is all about.

Safety and protection are among our most basic needs. A moving story that could be of great value and comfort is one that especially impacted my wife and me because it involved our daughter. You don't want to miss it!

I couldn't resist a chapter on marriage, starting with how this confirmed bachelor got there—and happy no less. Also, I share three powerful stories of marriages that were falling apart or about to which were completely transformed. In one case, the couple had been separated for a few years. In each situation, when one of the spouses saw what hadn't been seen before, something dramatic happened.

Is anyone going through depression, loneliness, or a lack of hope that seems to never end? Take heart! When you read my sister Carol's story, you will come to know that it is NEVER too late for something amazing to happen. Doctors tried various treatments and a lot of medications. That didn't work. It was a *Helping Hand* on more than one occasion that finally brought about the extraordinary breakthrough.

Another fantastic story I had the privilege of hearing is so compelling that I had to include it. It's about a man who spent most of his life as a homeless hobo, while doing a lot of harm to himself and others. It should cut through anybody's concerns about whether their lives can amount to anything meaningful or have purpose.

Problems and challenges will come. We rented out our house without a property manager and lived 1,800 miles away. Then, the morning after a new tenant moved in, his brother called to explain that our house was flooded, and the tenant was in the ER because he smashed his head trying to turn off the water. The next call was the girlfriend who said she was ankle-deep in water. Then the estranged wife called to say she just arrived at the house. Are you kidding?

One evening, servers and chefs in the restaurant kitchen were cursing. Suddenly, all eyes were on me, and someone said that if anyone could handle them, it was Stephen. A reservation was on the books for a couple who drove everyone crazy. They always had several outrageous demands, like asking the chef to go to the store if he didn't have a certain vegetable. Then they left a close-fisted tip. I accepted the challenge. You won't believe how it turned out.

Or how about the time I was pouring Dom Perignon champagne for a private party honoring arguably the most popular first lady in the world at that time. As I poured her glass, I said something to her. She immediately grabbed my hand, and a collective gasp from the guests filled the air. At the same time, the two bodyguards reached for their guns. What a surprise ending that had!

My second trip to Africa was with a few friends to Accra, Ghana. We were guests in a home, and the host explained that a severe water crisis had impacted the region, which could have very serious consequences. He asked me to go to the American Embassy to appeal for water. The ambassador told me that I must be crazy. As I stood still, without saying a word, something dramatic beyond my pay grade happened. Everything changed.

It may become clear that NO way could these stories (there are many more) have happened by chance. That's part of why I believe they are meant to be shared. You are a unique individual with special gifts and talents that were given to benefit you and impact others. It is my desire that this book provides the keys to open the doors of hope, encouragement, and life-changing power for your journey. Are you ready? Let's go!

PART ONE

MY SURPRISE JOURNEY

CHAPTER 1

I THOUGHT I WAS THERE BUT I WASN'T

"We're going to crash into the ocean, and Stephen, when I tell you, go to the back of the plane, kick open the door, and get out!" On August 3, 1964, my uncle Herbert Walker and I were flying a rebuilt WWII twin-engine Beechcraft on a pitch-black night over the west coast of Africa. I asked him how he planned to get out when the water came rushing in, and he said, "Don't worry about me. Just get the shark repellant and take care of yourself."

I immediately experienced overwhelming fear, hopelessness, and anger, beyond what words can describe. I lost it, and with a clear picture of my mother at my funeral wearing a black armband, I started swinging my fists at him, screaming, "You're killing me!" I could not have imagined the events leading up to that moment and what followed.

At two years old, I vividly remember wearing a chocolate-brown outfit and standing with my grandmother across the street from the hospital during the birth of my brother, Michael. I felt great anxiety, resentment, and jealousy. Sibling rivalry is not uncommon, but bickering lasting twenty-eight years is not good.

The sibling war had at least one ceasefire in 1949 when Michael was stricken with polio during the epidemic which caused many lives to be lost. He was given a 10 percent chance to live. Amazingly, he recovered. I went to the hospital with Dad to pick him up. On the way home, my brother and I sat in the back seat, and I had both of my arms wrapped around him. That made my dad cry.

Around age five, a fascinating event took place over several nights as I was in bed getting ready to go to sleep. Lights out and wide awake with my head on the pillow, I would look up toward the ceiling and get a clear visual image in my mind's eye of lots of people moving around and having a good time. Though I couldn't see any faces, I was aware of much activity and excitement. I had no doubt that the people I "saw" were in a different place than me. My parents never talked about spiritual things around the house, yet I remember saying, "God, what's going on up there?" Each time this occurred, my curiosity was stirred to the point that I would ask the same question but got no answer. On one occasion, I was so excited and eager to find out that I said, "God, I'm willing to trade my life down here for what's going on up there!" No reply. I felt no fear when I made the offer, and, if anything, I felt disappointed that I couldn't join "the party."

A few years later, I had recurring cold-sweat nightmares centered on a terrible fear of getting married. My parents would have to calm me down and assure me that I didn't have to get married. I didn't know where that fear came from, especially since my parents, aside from typical squabbles and making up quickly, seemed to have a regular, content marriage. Fortunately, the episodes finally went away.

My parents planned for me to have an orthodox bar mitzvah at age thirteen to honor my mother's father, who had started a Jewish synagogue in the Bronx. The usual timeframe to prepare is six months; however, they had me go for two years. During my studies, I learned to read and write Hebrew. They also taught many stories about Jewish history. When the rabbi read about the exodus of the Jews enslaved in Egypt, I had a mildly mystical experience when I heard the instructions Moses gave to the people. He told them they had to slaughter an innocent lamb and smear some of the blood over the doorposts of their houses. In that way, the coming angel of death would pass over them. At that moment, I vividly felt a warm aliveness from deep inside me, unlike anything I had felt before. Then I had a powerful impression that there was something much more to the story.

Just before I started high school, we moved to the fine suburb of Roslyn, Long Island. By then, Dad, who had started his own business, was doing very well. For me, it was golf at the country club, a live-in maid, and my own new Chevy convertible. Our neighbors, who owned the legendary Colony Record Shop in Manhattan, invited our family to their son's bar mitzvah. The impressive guest list

My bar mitzvah, holding Torah

included baseball great Mickey Mantle, Sammy Davis Jr. and Billy Daniels, who were starring in Broadway's Golden Boy, and the world-famous Killer Joe Dance Team.

My dad worked many long, hard hours. Mom was often out shopping or at the country club, doing her thing. I guess I needed to find some ways to get attention. The late, renowned Michael Crichton was in my history class, and, fortunately, he said NO when I asked if I could copy from him on a test. Also, an intercom announcement for me to go to the principal's office occurred nearly every week in my homeroom class. Each time, everyone would laugh, wondering how I would get out of it. I usually did.

When we first moved to Roslyn, I shared a bedroom with my brother, Michael. After many protests, I finally got my own bedroom. It had no window shades or covers, and the bright sun would wake me up very early. I complained profusely, to no avail, so I spray-painted the window black. When my mother walked in, she took off one of her shoes and sent it crashing through the window. It was a frigid winter, and I was so upset that I intentionally left my door open, causing the heating bills to go way up—payback. One morning, I was under a bunch of blankets when my mother and sister Carol came in. Mom said, "Oh my God, maybe he's dead."

Carol said, "Do you think he could survive under all that snow?"

I then realized that a heavy snowstorm had taken place during the night and covered me, so I remained very still as they were going through panic and guilt, loving every moment. When Mom said, "I'm responsible for killing him; it's all my fault," I stuck my head out of the blankets, and she gasped and turned pale. Soon after, there were shades on the windows.

Smoking pot was the cool social thing to do while I was in high school. So, of course, I jumped in. During that time, I had an emergency appendectomy. When my mom came to the hospital and asked if there was anything that needed to be done for me at home, I asked her to please water my marijuana plants that I had been secretly growing in the backyard. She actually agreed. What a nice mom!

Life then was so carefree that I stayed home and attended Hofstra College (now Hofstra University). Another craze at the time was taking LSD. I did my second trip with some friends, and it was so potent that we all felt like we could completely lose it. I called a psychiatrist friend in New York City who invited us to come over so he could keep an eye on us. It was nighttime. I was driving on the Long Island Expressway when suddenly I let out a terrified scream, "Help, I can only see two dimensions! The road looks like a TV." The thought of crashing flashed through my mind. Fortunately, my friends were able to guide me off the road so someone else could drive. It was a long and strange night. I never did that again.

At Hofstra, the cafeteria was the place to hang out. I noticed a guy with very long hair who wore the loudest clothing outfits of anyone around. At that time, it really stood out. I was curious to know his story, so I introduced myself. It turned out he was an aspiring actor taking some courses in the drama department. Plus, he was very intelligent. We became friends. I was concerned that this struggling actor did not starve. I would sometimes invite him over to my house to feed him lunch. Once in a while, I would bring him to the country club for some encouragement. We made a little fun bet on the putting green. I won and told him that, of course, he didn't have to pay. He insisted.

One day, someone approached me in the cafeteria who referred to my actor friend and said he noticed I was hanging around with a rich kid. I took offense and said that just because this guy didn't have much money, they shouldn't put him down. Then he asked if I had ever been to his house. I hadn't and assumed from the way he looked that he was living in a little studio apartment. When I asked, he invited me to his home. I was beyond shocked! His family lived in a very exclusive area on the water, with a huge, magnificent yacht right in the backyard dock. On the walls in the house were original Rembrandt and Van Gogh paintings. He told me how much he appreciated that I liked him as a friend, not knowing his family background, which I then kept under the radar.

Throughout college, I had no job, no social security card, no responsibility, and no accountability. I vowed never to work, thinking life was so good, why bother? I also had the ability to socialize easily. I thought I was *THERE*.

My uncle, nicknamed Tailspin Tommy, was a WWII Flying Tigers hero and barnstormer. In his air show finales, he would intentionally crash planes into walls and buildings (twenty-three intentional, twenty-seven total crashes). I idolized my flamboyant uncle. In 1964, Lord Malcolm Douglas-Hamilton of the UK royal family arranged with my uncle to fly one of two rescue mission planes to Premier Moïse Tshombe in the Belgian Congo, where countless people were being killed during the Congo revolutions. It was the summer between my junior and senior years. My uncle invited me to go along with his friend, Joe Walton, who was a private pilot. I was thrilled and thought it would be a chance-of-a-lifetime adventure.

I was living in a bubble, and if I'd had any awareness of reality, I would have caught several clues along the way beforehand and never have gone. A few months before the trip, my uncle took his lady friend and me to an airfield in Blairstown, New Jersey. The plan was that she was going to make her first parachute jump, and then we would all go to another airfield to see an airshow. After she landed, my uncle turned to me and said, "You're next." That was a complete shock, and how I let him talk me into putting on a parachute with no training or warning remains beyond me. I jumped using a ripcord that automatically opened the chute when I got out. The ride down was exhilarating; however, the excitement upon landing lasted only a moment. As soon as I tried to get up, I realized my knee was injured, which turned out to be torn ligaments. That required six weeks on crutches.

My parachute jump—no warning, no training, torn
knee ligaments, six weeks on crutches

While waiting for the planes to be upgraded with the required modifications for long-distance travel, something very bizarre happened. One day while listening to my car radio, the announcer said the broadcast was coming from Roberts Field in Monrovia, Liberia. It was eerie and portended life and death situations to follow. I later learned that radio waves could be reflected to earth from the ionosphere by a phenomenon called "skip."

My parents, who were reading about all the horrors happening there, vehemently protested my going. The battle got so heated that I had to be rushed to a doctor with an emergency nosebleed. My parents and I agreed to follow the doctor's advice on whether to make the trip. Unfortunately, he said I was so stressed out from thinking I wouldn't get to go that it would be better if I went. Soon after, I got a severe flu which kept me down for a week. I had never had the flu in summer. It did, however, likely wind up saving my life.

The planes required several months to rebuild. In order to fly long distances over water, the eight passenger seats in the cabin were removed and replaced with four 55-gallon drums for fuel. So, Lord Malcolm, his son Niall, and Ina Blitz, a girl I had arranged to go, left a week before us on the other plane. Our first stop was Gander, Newfoundland, and we landed at night with one engine out. The front strut (shock absorber) was damaged and took a few days to fix. When I was told that we would sleep on a metal bench on the airport hangar floor instead of at a hotel, I realized the trip would be very different from what I had imagined.

The next stop would be an eleven-hour trip over the ocean to the Azores in the Atlantic Ocean. After all the cabin gas barrels were filled, a gas leak occurred. While Joe Walton was working on the repairs, my uncle said to make sure there were no sparks; otherwise, we'd all be blown sky-high. More reality was setting in. Even with full reserve tanks, we were still below minimum fuel reserves. We learned that Lord Malcolm had chosen to go via Greenland and Iceland, which required much less fuel. I appealed to my uncle to take the same route; however, he took stubbornness to a new level and insisted on the way he had planned. We left in the dark in a no-visibility storm. The plane was so overweight that I had to move from my seat in the back and completely drape myself over the gas cans in the pilot's cabin.

Joe Walton is fixing a dangerous gas leak before our long ocean trip. The cabin seats were replaced with barrels of fuel.

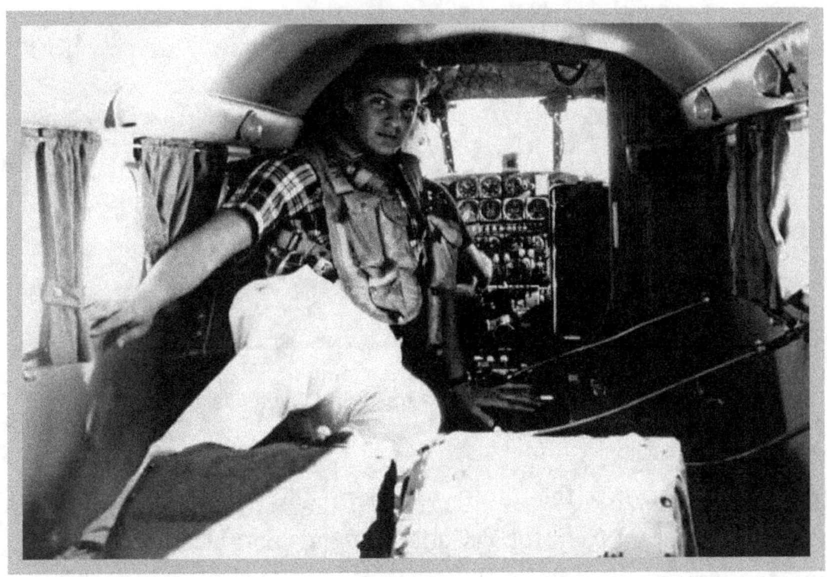

The plane was so overweight at takeoff from Gander,
Newfoundland, that I had to move from the rear seat and drape
myself over fuel barrels!

EVEN THEN, we used all the runway to barely get off the ground and couldn't climb over 700 feet. Suddenly, all five of our radios went out, and Joe and I were told that it was all over if they didn't come back on by themselves or if we got blown off course. Surely my uncle knew what to do. Words can't describe my hopeless feeling when he said it was beyond his control. Joe, an experienced pilot, insisted I go up to the copilot seat so he could go to the back to take tranquilizers. Death was staring us in the face. After five-plus very long hours, my uncle attempted to call a radar ship (Ocean Station Delta), and, to our total shock and amazement, the radios spontaneously came back on. They confirmed we were still on course and wouldn't die. Escape From Death #1.

Me flying copilot between the Azores and Canary Islands in the
Atlantic

WE NEVER FOUND the radio problem, and we encountered no issues in the next two stops (Canary Islands and Dakar). However, in another no-visibility storm between Dakar, Senegal, and Monrovia, Liberia, we lost all the radios again, and this time they did NOT come back. We flew five and a half hours using the compass course of our pre-flight plan. We did not know where we were or anything about changes in wind direction. If there was no cloud break or we drifted into a mountain, life was over. I was terrified. With zero visibility, we descended to 3,000, 2,000, 1,000 feet. Fear overwhelmed me. We had about one minute to find out if we would survive. In a surreal moment, we broke out of the clouds at 600 feet in direct line with the runway of Spriggs Payne Airport on the outskirts of Monrovia. In those conditions, the odds of that happening were virtually zero! I desperately wanted to land and recover; however, my uncle continued flying for another twenty minutes to land at Roberts Field International Airport. That airport was the very place from where I had strangely heard the radio broadcast in my car before the trip. Escape #2.

In the airport tower, we were told that Lord Malcolm's plane had left from that airport a week earlier, was missing, and had assumably crashed! While reviewing Malcolm's flight plan, my uncle saw 13,000-foot Mt. Cameroon (usually covered with clouds) on the tower's map that was NOT on our map. Then he told me that the next day he had planned to take the same route to Douala, Cameroon, and we probably would have had the same fate. If my uncle hadn't chosen to land at Roberts Field, we would not have known until it was too late. I had to be rushed to the infirmary for tranquilizers to calm my fears and guilt! We stayed overnight, and a man who heard about what had happened invited us to be guests in his home. He had a television, and some kids from the neighborhood came by to watch one of the first available programs in the area. They were so cute and fascinated by what they saw that I felt a momentary break from all the stress. Then an adult neighbor came in. He pulled my uncle and me aside to warn us that our host was an escapee from the Nazi regime. My uncle and I took turns staying awake all night. I couldn't make this stuff up! Escape #3.

Joe Walton's final destination was Monrovia, so then it was just my uncle and me. We changed our plans to go further down the coast to avoid Douala. It was nighttime as we approached Libreville, Gabon. The tower attendant told us the airport had closed without warning and that the nearest open airport was Douala. We asked him to shoot up red flares, which we never saw. My uncle confirmed what I already knew—we didn't have enough fuel to get there and were going to crash. That's when I lost it and started swinging my fists and screaming. I was out of control when words unexpectedly came up from deep inside me: "God, if you get me down from here alive, I'll do anything you want!" I had no idea where that came from or who I was talking to.

To my complete surprise, the clouds parted like the Red Sea. In the middle of my uncle trying to contain my hysteria and fly the plane, I did a double-check on the five empty gas tanks, and when I turned the dial to the last one, the gauge moved a little, which gave a glimmer of hope. It was all a blur. We touched down in Douala on fumes, and as soon as we landed, the storm clouds returned. We were then informed that was the first cloud opening in two weeks! I kissed the ground with copious tears pouring down my face. Although I sensed something beyond had happened to save our lives, I was in deep shock. Escape #4.

In Douala, we met Malcolm's brother, the Duke of Hamilton, and two other family members. They were part of a search party for the missing plane, which sadly was found two years later. We then flew to our final destination, Leopoldville in the Congo. Just to add a little drama as we were landing, my uncle cut in front of a plane riddled with bullet holes in the engines. He was angrily scolded by the tower attendant. Welcome to the Congo! By then, I was a basket case and declined the invitation to meet with Premier Tshombe.

Search team for Lord Malcolm Hamilton's missing plane: Uncle Herbert (left), Ambassador Edward Warner (3rd from left), me (center), Duke of Hamilton (on my left), and other family members

Details in French of the plane search

Uncle Herbert meeting with Belgian Congo Premier Moïse
Tshombe

My uncle and me in the Congo with workers from Sabena Airlines

After returning home, I learned that the search story was all over the international news, and my parents hadn't known if I was still alive. Then came my gut-wrenching call to the mother of the girl I had sent on the other plane to say that her daughter wouldn't be coming back. I don't think I even realized at the time how much it affected me that I lived and she died. The toll of these horrific events started a nine-year downhill spiral in my life.

Nephews of Lost Peer Search Cameroon Peak

Special to The New York Times

DOUALA, Cameroon, Aug. 13—Two nephews of the missing Lord Malcolm Douglas-Hamilton set off to scale the 13,350-foot Cameroon Mountain today with fading hopes of finding a trace of their uncle's plane. It disappeared more than three weeks ago on a flight to the Congo.

Diarmaid Douglas-Hamilton, 24 years old, who is enrolled at Harvard Graduate School this fall, and his brother, Iain, 21, an Oxford student, left their base camp at Buea this morning. They were led by an African guide and four porters.

The 55-year-old former Conservative Member of Parliament was an accomplished pilot with more than 7,000 hours' flying time, most of it with the Royal Air Force. During World War II he was awarded the Distinguished Flying Cross. He recently lived in the United States at 25 Ives Road, Hewlett, L. I.

Also missing are Lord Malcolm Douglas-Hamilton's son, Niel, 22, who was co-pilot, and Joy Blitz, a teacher from New York who was hitching a lift.

August 14, 1964 *New York Times* article (one of many) about missing plane search

CHAPTER 2

How Far Down Could I Go?

The following semester, a fraternity brother approached me with a scheme to avoid the draft during the Vietnam War by paying a fee to his friend on the draft board. I said NO every time he approached me! Finally, the emotion of having been part of someone else losing their life got to me, and I didn't want to kill anyone, so I agreed, and my draft status changed.

After college, my dad shocked me by saying I had to work. Me work? His friend was head of the photography studio at Macy's department store in New York City. He took it upon himself to get me a job at the studio cleaning and sweeping. I took the Long Island railroad to do something that felt so demeaning to me. From my spoiled, entitled background, that job felt like an episode of *Dirty Jobs*. After a few months, I told my father it was getting to me.

Then my dad arranged job interviews for me at two life insurance agencies. I accepted a position with Paul Goodman at his successful life insurance agency on Madison Avenue in New

York City. Things went well, and I achieved Leaders Club in my first year.

One morning around 7:00 a.m., I was awakened by two FBI agents knocking on my bedroom door. When they came in, they informed me a warrant was out for my arrest for draft dodging. I later found out that my dad saw them at the front door on his way to work, let them in, then left! They drove me to FBI headquarters, where there were crowds of reporters and thirty-plus other young men who had been arrested. It turned out to be the largest draft-dodging bust in history, and the story was plastered all over TV and the front page of newspapers. We were all released that day, and I rationalized it was just a scare tactic.

New York World-Telegram

The Sun

Local Forecast: Cloudy tonight becoming fair tomorrow. Details on Page 2

38 on Draft-Dodging List

In the crackdown today on alleged participants in a draft-dodging scheme, arrest warrants were issued for the following persons on charges of evading the draft:

BARASH, Neil S., 23, 2230 Motte Ave., Far Rockaway, Queens.

DUCKMAN, Michael N., 18, Heights Rd., Manhasset, L.I.

ECKHAUS, Mark S., 21, 50 Woodmere Blvd., Woodmere, L.I.

FERRER, John, 20, 23 W. 106th St.

FREIBERG, Jacob, 22, 1138 Foam Pl., Far Rockaway, Queens.

FUTTERMAN, Alexander C., 21, 164-11 45th Ave., Flushing, Queens.

GHELBERG, Lewis Henry, 23, 78-45 220th St., Bayside, Queens.

GRATTEL, Melvyn P., 22, 7 Jordan Drive, Great Neck, L.I.

GRAZIANO, Vito, 23, 459 Henry St., Bklyn.

GUTERMAN, Gerald, 23, 46 Schenck Ave., Great Neck, L.I.

HOLUB, Jack D., 21, 215 West Hudson St., Long Beach, L.I.

KAMISAROFF, Barry I., 20, 699 W. 239th St., Bronx.

KARPEN, Robert, 19, 512 Beach 66th St., Arverne, Queens.

KNOBEL, Steven Barry, 22, 385 Beach 12th St., Far Rockaway, Queens.

LIANTONIO, Leonardo, 20, 112 Jefferson St., Hoboken, N.J.

LUIZZA, Anthony T., 22, 86-40 80th St., Woodhaven, Queens.

MARGO, Mitchell Stuart, 18, 2801 Ocean Parkway, Flushing, Queens.

MAYERSOHN, Ronald Ames, 23, 103 Combs Ave., Woodmere, L.I.

PATERNOSTRO, Alfred Peter, 22, 162-13 77th Rd., Flushing, Queens.

RICH, Stephen D., 20, 1150 Brighton Beach Ave., Bklyn.

SCHULMAN, Neil I., 19, 246 Echo Pl., Bronx.

SEMENSOHN, Saul, 20, 188-02A 71st Crescent, Fresh Meadows, Queens.

VANDINA, Robert J., 22, 918 Balfour St., Valley Stream, L.I.

WALKER, Stephen, 22, 180 Beach Dr., Roselyn Heights, L.I.

WEISBLUM, Howard, 22, 605 Beach Lane, Far Rockaway, Queens.

GUTERMAN, Rubin, 59, 19 Bonnie Dr., Westbury, L.I.

HOLUB, Allan, 50, 215 West Hudson St., Long Beach, L.I.

KAPLAN, Stuart, 22, 8 Laurett Lane, Freeport, L.I.

LUIZZA, James, 47, 86-40 80th St., Woodhaven, Queens.

MILLER, Paul George, 28, 98-32 57th Ave., Rego Park, Queens.

PATERNOSTRO, John, 45, 161-13, 77th Rd., Flushing, Queens.

RISCH, Sidney, 60, 1150 Brighton Beach Ave., Bklyn.

SCHULMAN, Julian, 50, 246 Echo Pl., Bronx.

WINTNER, Philip, 54, 392 Felter Ave., Hewlett, L.I.

Arrest warrants were issued for the following persons on charges of aiding and abetting:

ECKHAUS, Morton M., 50 Woodmere Blvd., Woodmere, L.I.

FELDMAN, Robert, 25, 439 Beach 22nd St., Far Rockaway, Queens.

FREIBERG, Leon, 1138 Foam Pl., Far Rockaway, Queens.

GOTTFRIED, Solomon, 56, 2 Elvet Lane, Levittown, L.I.

Front page article on day of arrest-all over TV as
well

In January 1967, my uncle invited me to fly as copilot on a twin-engine Cessna from New York to Mineral Wells, Texas. I was already a single-engine certified pilot. The hook was that I would get free instruction in a multi-engine plane. Unfortunately, I took the bait. What's the definition of insanity? You'd think I'd learn. At the time, I was dating an attractive model with long blond hair. I invited her to go along, and she accepted.

A few hours into the trip, my uncle quietly said we were losing both engines. I didn't take him seriously because that was his sense of humor. But when I looked at the instruments, I realized he wasn't kidding. Now what? We were over a populated area. He then explained that he had just radioed Quantico Marine Base to call in a mayday emergency landing. I asked if we were going to make it, and he said we would try. Although my uncle was a legendary pilot, well-trained for these situations, that wasn't very reassuring.

It is strange flying a twin-engine plane with no sound. We glided for some time, and when he finally pointed out the airfield in the distance, I began to get a sense of hope. As we got closer, I noticed crowds of people on both sides of the runway and said there must be a big event. My uncle replied that those were the firefighters and medical team in case we crashed and caught fire. Whoa!

The landing was perfect. When we got out of the plane to cheers and applause from the first responders, that's when I knew the seriousness of the situation. My girlfriend was tall and wearing a purple micro-mini skirt. When she got out of the plane, it sounded like the roars had stepped up several decibels. Funny thing, we got speedy attention getting our plane repaired! Escape #5.

I moved into a nice off-Fifth-Avenue brownstone. Though internal struggles continued, I committed to working hard at my new job. With Paul Goodman's help in closing a large deal, I won the Man-of-the-Year award at his agency. One of the perks of winning the award was a photo op and credit in the *New York Times*. I showed up with long hair wearing a robe like the

Maharishi, who was made famous by The Beatles. Of course, I should have worn a suit and tie. The company decided it was better to pass on the photo and article.

Troubled Times

Then, two years after my arrest, a notice for the trial came. My attorney said the plea deal available was to join the Army and no prison. I agreed. However, on sentencing day, the judge said, "Four years in the federal penitentiary," and I was immediately taken to West Street Jail in handcuffs! I went into severe shock, and the next three days seemed like an eternity. I thought if there were a hell, it would be something like that. I was then transferred by bus to Lewisburg Medium Security Prison (Lewisburg, Pennsylvania) while handcuffed to a six-foot-six-inch draft prisoner for seven hours. This facility has been home to some very high-profile crime figures, and, during that long week, someone pointed out Jimmy Hoffa. I remember once while standing in one of the two food lines, I became aware that everyone in the room was intensely staring at me with a terrifying look. Then I realized (no one had told me) that one line was for black inmates and one for white.

The draft prisoners were then taken to Allenwood Minimum Security Prison (Allenwood, Pennsylvania). We were told it was from here we could apply for our Army physical to enlist. It sounded like the process would take a few weeks, but as the months went by, I descended into a state of deep depression and fear. I couldn't function and regularly went to the prison psychiatrist, who prescribed tranquilizers. We slept on double-decker bunk beds, and my bunkmate was an Irish Green Beret who got put in prison because he was overzealous to kill the enemy in the Vietnam War. I offered him my pills so he wouldn't kill me, and he accepted. That was a huge relief. However, another inmate told me that two guys were planning to take me out, and I thought it was all over. Then I heard they escaped, got caught, and were put in a different prison. That was just beyond belief. I asked myself if it was possible someone *up there* could be looking out for me? Escape #6.

After five long months, we were finally taken to enlist in the Army. The last step of the physical was medical questions. The sergeant shouted, "Does anyone have any of the following?" Instantly, one of the most surreal experiences of my life took place. A "pair of hands" under each of my arms lifted me out of my chair, yet no one was near me! I thought I had lost it, and although I sat right back down, the sergeant screamed and demanded to know why I stood. I didn't know what to say except that I had been checked for an irregular heartbeat many years before, and it was determined I was fine. He pulled me aside and brought in a cardiologist who diagnosed me with a heart condition. They sent me back to prison to serve the rest of my sentence. I experienced intense despair and devastation, and on the next visit from my family, I talked to my brother about getting me sleeping pills.

A few weeks later, I was surprised when my father and a friend flew in a private plane to pick me up, explaining that the judge had paroled me to do community service at the Grand Street Settlement House. My job was to tutor a few kids who were struggling in school. I wasn't functioning well and was sometimes late, which led to a violation of probation with a new trial. Things looked bleak, so we appealed to have me go in for psychological evaluation. The judge agreed, and the report summary read: "Stephen is in urgent need of help; he could self-destruct at any moment." We then asked if I could be released to work in my father's business. Fortunately, that touched the judge's heart because he could relate to his own son. On an encouraging note, I found out later that the kids I had tutored got passing grades, and their families were most grateful.

Still dealing with much internal turmoil, I tried covering it up with ongoing all-night parties and getting high. That meant smoking pot to cover up the pain and even doing speed a few times. I had very scary incidents with both of those, which made me realize I was playing around with life and death. One time I was so high on pot, I found myself sitting by my apartment window waiting for aliens to come and rescue me. When I realized what was happening, I was terrified and never did marijuana again. I understand that these days pot is much more potent and could lead to complete breakdowns or worse. On another occasion, I was at a party, high on speed. I got such an excruciating pain in my chest that I thought I was having a heart attack. My immediate reaction was that if I survived, I would never do speed again. I survived. I stopped.

My friends knew some of the top music groups, and I got to hang out with The Who, including being a backstage guest at the Tanglewood Music Festival. Although I didn't go, I even had an invitation to meet and party with The Beatles. But nothing took away the pain inside. Due to extreme stress and guilt, I went back and forth to doctors for severe low blood sugar, ulcers, and other stomach issues. Also, I had a collapsed lung three times, the last of which required major surgery. When the attending doctor told me he would get me a resident, I almost lost it. I told him I wanted the best there was and the doctor he would choose if it was his son. He said, in that case, it would be Dr. Paul Ebert, the new chief of surgery. Over the next few years, during routine medical checkups, I was told the surgery was so good that doctors couldn't even tell it had been done.

Things got so bad for me that I had a brick wall built over my apartment bedroom window without permission, disconnected the doorbell, and had three locks on the door. When a fire in the building happened, I never heard the firefighters ringing to evacuate. When my mother came to visit and saw the brick wall, she ran out screaming, "You're back in prison!" And I was. One day, I felt so angry about my life that I looked up, shook my fist, and said, "God, whoever you are, I hate you!" Then I used a calculator to figure out how many hours of suffering there would be if I lived to different ages.

CHAPTER 3

"No, No, It Can't Be That!"

After the judge released me to work in my father's business, my brother Michael also came to work with us. It was extremely intense and demanding with high-pressure deadlines. Michael couldn't handle the stress and left town. Dad was so grieved that he wore a black armband as if my brother was dead. Michael called after a few weeks, then came home for a visit. My dad wouldn't go to the airport, so my mom, sister Carol, and I went to pick him up. He looked like a completely different person, and I noticed people in the airport were staring at him. I was jealous. To cope, I rationalized that when he got home and my dad got upset, he'd be back to his old self. He walked in and said, "Dad, I love you," and they wound up on the floor crying in each other's arms. Seeing that shocked me because I don't recall ever hearing those words growing up, let alone hugs and tears.

Michael didn't say what had happened to him, but he invited me to visit him in Los Angeles. That was another surprise because we had been at odds with each other from the time he was born. After being released from probation, I decided to go and connected with a college buddy who invited me to stay with him in his ocean-view Malibu apartment. Instead of looking at the beautiful scenery, I kept my room dark. I still felt utterly lost and all alone. Michael would come by from time to time and ask me if I wanted to meet his friends. I always said no. One day he came over for a visit and asked me why I didn't want to meet anyone. At that point, I broke down in tears and said, "It's undeniable something has happened to you. If I go and it doesn't happen to me, I'll feel like all hope is gone."

I then wound up in the hospital with a thyroid condition requiring medication for life. The doctors said if I stopped taking the pills, my system could shut down. I was on the verge of a breakdown, and my mom flew out to be with me.

Michael invited us to a birthday party at a beautiful house his friends were renting in the Hollywood Hills that they called "the castle." I reluctantly agreed to go, thinking my mom would protect me. The host was a retired heart surgeon known as Doc. His radiant smile rattled my cage. My first words to him were, "I'm sorry, you make me a nervous wreck," and he smiled even more.

A few days later, Michael wanted to show us the magnificent home overlooking the ocean that his friends had just purchased. It turned out, unbeknownst to Michael, that Doc and his assistant Marilyn were there, which made me uncomfortable. But Doc was very gracious. He shared many amazing stories. I didn't understand why they seemed to disturb me at my core. The more he spoke, the more I found myself sliding down my chair until I was practically under the table. Then, he suddenly looked at me and said I was beyond words reaching me and needed to have an experience of God. That was the first time he mentioned that name, and it shook me so badly, I wanted to leave.

As we were near the front door, Doc asked my mother that since her father was a rabbi, would it be okay if he prayed for her in the name of the God of Abraham, Isaac, and Jacob. My thought was he knew we were Jewish, that he was a con man wanting our money, and we'd better get out, but my mom agreed. As Doc was praying, she started swaying, and I ran to rescue her. Doc then asked if he could pray for me, and I explained that I needed to leave immediately. He just smiled, and I calculated that I'd be out the door in one minute if I let him pray. So, I agreed. He reached out his hand near me and prayed in a very bold, authoritative voice: "As in the time of Moses, those who were for God stepped forward, and those against fell backward. Lord, Stephen needs to feel your touch right now. I ask this in the name of the Holy One of Israel, blessed be His name."

I had never seen or heard anything like that. A thought immediately came that I was going to fall forward. My knees got so wobbly that I wound up flat on my face on the beautiful carpet in the middle of the marble floor, wailing profusely for a long time. At one point, I looked up and went right back down, sobbing. When I finally got up, somewhat embarrassed, I felt like a huge weight had been lifted.

I am grateful for Dr. Selwyn McCabe and his assistant Marilyn Berger, without whom I may not be here today.

From the moment I left, I tried to understand what had taken place. A few days later, I was in my car at a traffic light when something fascinating happened. What felt like a big bubble formed and worked its way up from my stomach area. Then, without me doing anything, out of my mouth came the sound, *Jhhh*. As I looked down and wondered how this bizarre event was happening, another sound like *Jeez* came out, and I reacted, saying, "No, no, it can't be that!" It happened a third time, and out of my mouth came the name, Jesus. Tears came rolling down my face, and I felt a tremendous peace and aliveness of life, unlike anything I had ever experienced! After a nine-year living nightmare, it was a soul awakening, and I knew: All Is Well. In that elevated state of clarity, my next thought was that wow, this revelation and freedom is for everyone!

I immediately turned my car around and drove twenty-five miles, hoping to see Doc. He had never mentioned that name, and I needed to find out what was going on. I excitedly walked right through the unlocked front door, and when I saw him, I ran up and asked, "Was what happened to me the other day… was it Jesus?" He threw his arms around me with tears in his eyes and said, "Yes, it is Jesus!" On top of feeling beyond wonderful, all my illnesses went away, including my need for thyroid pills!

Why was this so impactful and shocking to me? Several years ago, my mother reminded me (I had forgotten) that at age seven, I came home from a friend's house and said, "Jesus is my God." My parents instantly forbade me from ever saying the name Jesus again, as well as not allowing me to play with my friend. No wonder I had screamed, "No, no, it can't be that," as the sound *Jeez* started to come out of my mouth. When I asked her of all the things I had said in my life, why that had affected them so much, she responded, "Because we believed you," and further explained that it would have been a betrayal of her father, who was an Orthodox lay rabbi. She then told me they put me in Hebrew school an extra few years before my bar mitzvah to be deprogrammed.

Writing about this forty-eight years later brings a little different perspective. I had gotten to the point of running out of strength to go on. Then, in a very surreal moment, someone rescued me. I found out his name was Jesus, and there was no more need for despair or worry. I thought if I could audibly hear Him speaking to me at that time, it may have been something like this:

> Stephen, I knew you before you were born and have watched over you since birth. At an early age, I gave you a little hint of what's going on in Heaven. Then I made my name known to you. However, your family couldn't handle it. The enemy had a plan to kill you numerous times, and you were always rescued. You were willing to go into the military, and I redirected your path. I felt your pain and anger toward me, and when you were ready, I revealed myself in the way that was needed. When you were about to crash into the ocean over Africa, you said, "I'll do anything you want if you get me down from here alive." Now I'm going to take you where you weren't planning to go. It will be a life of service, giving, and caring for others. That's what I'm all about. I am going to prepare you for the many things I will send your way, so stay alert. These experiences will not be just for you but also to share with others.

Jesus was the "stranger" I didn't know who always knew me! He rescued me even after I threw my hatred and hurts at him.

PART TWO

How Does It Work in Jobs?

CHAPTER 4

WHAT'S LOVE GOT TO DO WITH IT?

Soon after my new life began, exciting things happened to me. A worldwide group asked me to go on a touring circuit and share my experience with others. However, I got good advice from Doc that I might do better first to get grounded in this newly found great love. I trusted that wisdom. He also explained his hope that as people worked on restoring the villa, their lives could be restored. Although working with my hands was not a part of my spoiled upbringing, I decided to jump in.

My practical education came fast. One of my former girlfriends came for a visit. I naïvely thought she wanted a new life. It wasn't that way at all, and she left. Then came another ex —wrong again, same result. When the third one came out for a visit, I thought surely it was my duty to help her. I introduced her to Doc and Marilyn and left for a few hours. When I came back, I asked Doc how things went. He had a mischievous smile and said something to the effect that he must have touched a spiritual nerve because she smacked him in the face. Feeling awful and embarrassed, I asked why these things with my old girlfriends kept happening. He said, "When you're in a war, you are allowed to duck the bullets." I got it! Funny thing, no more ex-girlfriends came to visit after that.

Now what? It's a practical world. How do you translate the experience into everyday jobs, relationships, and other areas? I didn't know where to start, so I got a job back in the life insurance industry, where I'd had prior success. My desk was in a small cubicle with no windows. One afternoon, another agent, Johnny Baker, asked to talk to me. We had only briefly spoken once a couple of weeks earlier. Johnny is African American and part American Indian. He said that he saw something in my eyes and told me he was searching for answers. His marriage, which included children, was falling apart. His life was a total mess. I smiled and said, "Oh, is that all?" I invited him to meet some of my friends that night. Johnny has a great gift of openheartedness and being real. He shared his pain and grief. We all got together several more times. He told us that he had looked in various directions, and nothing worked. He was feeling desperate, not wanting his marriage to end.

About the third evening, Johnny's heart opened, and he began sobbing profusely. That took an enormous amount of trust. His life changed in an instant. Although I was still single and all this was fairly new to me, I told Johnny that there should be a way to restore his marriage. I had not yet met Jo Ann. Shortly after that, Johnny got together with her. He poured his heart out and told her what a rotten husband he had been and that he loved her. Things turned around, and they got closer than ever. She individually, as well as together with Johnny, touched many lives over the next forty-five years. Jo Ann had a regal spirit. It was the power of love that broke down the walls inside Johnny. Only then could he see what he couldn't see. He had the power, freedom, and humility to win her back. Sadly, Jo Ann recently died of COVID, and we all miss her very much.

~

ALTHOUGH I HAD BEEN successful in the life insurance business in New York, it just wasn't the same for me, so I left that job. I had no clue what to do. Two of my friends worked as servers in an upscale seafood restaurant in Beverly Hills. Without my knowledge, they went to their boss and asked if I could train to be a server. When they approached me, I told them that I could not see myself wearing a uniform, punching a clock, and carrying trays, let alone waiting on customers. A few weeks later, they again approached me. I agreed to go through the motions with their assurance that no job was available. It was a very busy restaurant, and they worked in teams of two.

On my third night of training, a server didn't show up, and the boss was very concerned. Suddenly, all eyes were on me, and I had a pit in my stomach. A server pleaded for my help. He said to just do everything he would tell me, and I'd be okay. I shocked myself by saying yes just for that shift. I was so nervous, and the adrenaline was flowing. At the end of the night, my teammate told me I did so well that the boss was going to offer me a job. My worst fears had come upon me. I was desperate for an income and agreed, figuring I would find something else within a few weeks. That didn't happen, and I was then a full-time server, carrying those trays. The busboys would laugh at me because I was so nervous about dropping a tray on a customer. It was a big adjustment from thinking I would be an international speaker to the reality that my job was just to take care of whoever was in front of me.

Later on, I learned Doc had invented a heart bypass pump which could potentially benefit pediatric and adult cardiac surgery. Grateful for my new start in life, I offered to show the research system prototype to doctors, which I did on a part-time basis. So, it turned out that working in a restaurant afforded me the flexibility needed to pursue this.

Fast forward a few years. I was between jobs and applied for a position at Bernard's, a beautiful French restaurant inside the historic Biltmore Hotel in downtown Los Angeles. They had no captain or server jobs open; however, they offered me a part-time sommelier position. I asked what it meant. They explained that I would wear a wine tasting cup around my neck (tastevin), offer wine suggestions to the customers, and then taste the wine myself before pouring it for the guests. I said, "And I would get paid to do that?" When they said yes, I told them, "I'm in." They added that they thought I'd be perfect for the job. Explaining I knew virtually nothing about wine, they said not to worry because their other wine steward would train me. That was a surprise start of a new career.

Being a sommelier allowed me many more opportunities and time to connect with customers, which I love. The additional earnings were certainly a welcome change. I learned that the majority of people who work in the wine industry are very gracious and hospitable. Over the years, I developed many great friendships, which are so rewarding.

Everything went so well so quickly that, a few weeks later, I was hired as head sommelier at the exclusive L'Escoffier French restaurant in the penthouse of the Beverly Hilton Hotel in Beverly Hills. The service team included captains in tuxedos and servers. A customer favorite was the three-piece society band and dance floor.

TURNING WINE INTO A WEDDING

One evening, I approached a table and introduced myself to an older couple. The man smiled and said he was Judge Ralph Burns, retired Superior Court Judge of Beverly Hills, and introduced his wife, Mildred. He then explained it was their first time dining at L'Escoffier and that Mildred would like a glass of Robert Mondavi Fume Blanc. I replied, "I'm sorry, we don't serve that wine by the glass. Would you like something similar, or you could get a bottle and take the rest home?" He insisted she only liked that wine, and they didn't want to take anything home. A number of thoughts went through my mind. The wine is not very expensive, and I'm sure he could well afford it. Why not get the captain to come over since wine by the glass was his job? I guess I could have said that I would check with the manager, but I didn't think of that.

As I was leaving the table, he said, "Both of our first spouses died, and we remarried a few years ago. I really love her and just want her to be happy." That cut through all my logical thoughts. I felt this love he had for her and excitedly wanted to make it happen. Then I ran over to the manager and told him what I wanted to do. He said, "Of course, that's why we have you here because you care about the customers." When I presented the glass of wine with enthusiasm, it touched their hearts. The judge had tears in his eyes. They looked like young newlyweds, all smiles, grateful for the personal care. It was so sweet.

The judge and his wife became regulars. They played the role of parents by asking if I was married or if any prospects were on the horizon. I defensively would snap, "No." I explained that I had dated Becky for several years, proposed to her, she accepted, and I got so petrified that I backed out. And further, the both of us were in the same circle of friends but were barely speaking to one another. Each time in, the judge would ask if anything was happening in the marriage department. My response was that he must have met my parents, and they were paying him to do this. Then on one occasion, he said, "If you ever get married, my gift to you will be that I will do your ceremony." I expressed great appreciation for the kind offer and assured him nothing would happen for some time.

The following Valentine's Day, my friend, who was about to go on his honeymoon, challenged me to get flowers for Becky. That stirred in me how much I did love her. The fire soon rekindled, and we got engaged.

When Judge Burns and Mildred came back to the restaurant, I jumped in before they finished the usual marriage question, saying, "Yes, August 18th!" Although he didn't know anything about our situation, to my amazement, he immediately rattled off the exact same advice given to us to not start a marriage by going into debt with a big wedding. Imagine a Jewish judge in Beverly Hills saying NOT to spend money on a wedding… seriously?

On a beautiful summer day, Judge Burns, attired in his official black robe, and his wife Mildred, arrived at Becky's parents' condo in Sherman Oaks. The judge performed a personal and touching ceremony. They later invited us to be dinner guests in their home. Becky and I remain grateful for their sweet wedding gift, the wisdom of good advice that helped reassure us we had made the right decision, and a caring friendship with such fine people.

Our wedding was simple but special. One of my regular customers even gifted us with a fantastic bottle of wine, and the Hilton arranged for complimentary suites in both Lake Arrowhead and Palm Springs for our four-day honeymoon. Total cost: less than 100 dollars!

When the judge asked for a glass of wine that was not on the list, I offered alternative solutions, and he wasn't interested. It was only when he shared they were both recently remarried and expressed his love for her that everything changed. It would not have been the same if I had just routinely said I needed to check with the manager. It was a heart thing. The judge opened his heart, and when he saw the response from my heart, it made a big difference. That was the start of a wonderful relationship and an unexpected wedding gift. A little love, a little care, and look what happened. Who could have imagined that a glass of wine would turn into a wedding?

MARRIAGE WALLS CRUMBLE

Every Saturday, L'Escoffier brought in additional staff from the hotel's banquet department. On one of those evenings, a man I hadn't met before approached me and said, "There's something about you. I can see it in your eyes." That caught me off guard. From that point, we talked every Saturday as time permitted. He was very soft-spoken and gracious. He had married a beautiful woman about ten years younger than himself, who had left him several years before and was living in his house in Mexico with another man. In addition, he shared that he had just completed the Alcoholics Anonymous (AA) program. As he talked about the pain of the situation with his estranged wife, I realized a volcano of anger that could erupt at any time was underneath the calm surface. I told him it went even deeper than just being angry with his wife. I said that perhaps he was just mad at God, and he got very defensive. He said, "Please don't say that. I'll be punished." That's when I smiled and said, "Don't worry, He already knows, and you won't be punished."

I explained three options: 1) If his anger was taken out on the wife or boyfriend, there could be serious consequences; 2) If he allowed it to stay inside him, it could cause ongoing emotional trauma or eventually suicide; 3) He could get rid of it without doing any harm. I encouraged him to privately let it come up and then transfer (release) it to God, never to return, and suggested he could pound on some pillows if it got too intense.

One Saturday, he excitedly shared that he finally let his anger come to the surface and kept feeling more hatred toward his wife until he felt like he was going to explode. Then it broke, and he experienced unexpected rivers of love for her. I had tears in my eyes and was so happy for him. I told him he was a free man and no longer had to be in bondage to anger. As I walked away, he said there was more. He hadn't been in touch with his wife for a few years, but as he let go, she called him from Mexico saying how much she missed him! My jaw dropped. I asked if he understood what had happened, and he nodded yes. The last time I saw him, he was on his way to see his wife in Mexico, feeling like an excited young man in love going on a special date. He had a renewed hope for the future.

It's a phenomenon what can happen by trading in anger and bitterness. It was as if her problems and his problems no longer existed. The love that came pouring out was so pure and powerful that nothing else mattered.

SURPRISE ANNIVERSARY GIFT

After many years working in restaurants as a server and sommelier, I was offered a sales and management position as the Los Angeles District Manager of Family Entertainment Network. I gladly welcomed an opportunity in a new arena. The company had top-of-the-world animators who produced high-quality, accurate historical and biblical videos along with interactive books. Some weeks, my personal and team sales were number one in the country. The company was expanding and rolled out regional management (RM) positions around the country. I got offered the RM of Arizona; however, Becky did not want to move. I persisted, and finally, she gave in. Then came a jolt. With our furniture on a truck from Los Angeles to Arizona, I got word that the company had changed its mind and was withdrawing all management job offers. Thankfully, a few days later, they reversed their decision, and the job was back on for at least six months.

I quickly learned that I was walking into a hostile environment. One man was sure he was going to get the position, and he did everything in his power to convince everyone not to work for me so that I would have to leave. That was an extreme challenge, and I jumped in with everything I had. The products were typically sold at kiosks in malls or stores like Walmart, Sam's Club, etc. The animated videos would continuously play, which attracted customers to come by. My position included hiring and training salespeople and securing locations that would allow us to set up the displays. I was fortunate to hire some great people, and, as it turned out, some of the existing team decided they wanted to work with me as well. When I arrived, my region was ranked twenty-five of fifty-seven markets in the US. In about four months, both my personal sales and team sales brought us to the number one market in the country. In addition, the videos were produced in Spanish, and I was making connections to be the first in the company to go international by opening the market in Monterey, Mexico. Earnings were good, and business was growing. Then the company had its fast-growth struggles and pulled the entire management program from across the country. I instantly went from number one to no job!

The earnings program included a salary and commissions, which were complicated because my region had been selected for three test programs. When the job ended, I felt like I was still owed some money and spent many hours putting together the financial reports to support my claims. The company insisted they didn't owe me anything despite all my efforts. Losing a job and not getting paid all I thought was owed was quite painful. I decided not to fight the situation but just to let it go. I quickly found a modest maître d' job at a Marriott resort.

Several months went by, and our tenth wedding anniversary

was approaching. As a husband, I wanted to do something special, but since finances were tight, Becky and I planned a fun one-dollar movie night. A few days before, with tears in my eyes, I *looked up* and asked, "Is a one-dollar movie the best we can do?" Then I just dropped it.

On August 17, 1995, the day before our anniversary, a lady from my former company called and excitedly said, "Stephen, I'm so sorry it took so long (seven months), but I'm happy to tell you that we owe you money!" I had tears of joy as I explained to her that the next day was our tenth anniversary. She was so moved and said, "Please plan something special for your wife because I'm overnighting you a $1,700 check." Imagine a company that is struggling financially gets back in touch seven months after a review and decline of commissions and overnights payment in full! My efforts were rewarded. So, I quickly arranged for our kids to stay with friends, and the next day, I told Becky I had a surprise and to pack a bag. When we finally got near beautiful Sedona, Arizona, I told her what was happening.

It was a surprise gift for our tenth anniversary, and what a wonderful one it turned out to be. I love the lines from a song that Whitney Houston sang, "Hold on, he's on his way… he may not come when you want him but he's right on time." The timing couldn't have been better!

CHILDHOOD FRIENDSHIP RENEWED

I was very fortunate to get the head sommelier job at Del Frisco's Double Eagle Steak House in Las Vegas. It is a stand-alone, world-class restaurant with seven dining rooms and an impressive wine list. We would have up to three sommeliers on busier nights, each serving a separate section.

On one rare occasion, I was asked to take care of another sommelier's table. As I approached, I heard the guests talking about Joplin, one city in Missouri where Becky had lived. Throughout my years in restaurant service, I had met quite a few people from Missouri and would usually make casual conversation telling them my wife was from there. On that night, I called Becky and let her know about the party from Joplin. She asked me to see if they knew Polly Klein. One of the ladies said, "You mean Polly Greer, who used to be Polly Klein before she got married? Yes, we know her." I called Becky again to give her the report, and she asked me to please get Polly's number. I made the connection. Polly and Becky were close childhood friends and hadn't seen each other in many years. I was not aware that Becky had recently been trying to locate Polly. She later told me she had gotten to the point of giving up and made a prayerful appeal for help. She was thrilled when they finally spoke and learned that some things she had done for Polly greatly impacted her life. When Becky and I moved from Tennessee in January 2012, we drove cross-country and stopped in Joplin. It was a heartfelt rendezvous for Becky and Polly, and the girls enjoyed meeting each other's husbands.

We had seen TV news clips of an EF5 tornado with 200 mph winds that had hit Joplin on May 22, 2011, killing 161, injuring 1,150, and flattening nearly 1,000 homes and structures. Polly drove us around the city. Seeing firsthand the size and scope of the aftermath was chilling and sobering. In addition to all the devastation, Polly told us about an amazing, unique phenomenon known as "The Butterfly People of Joplin." In every case, as a family was facing imminent death, the young children saw what they described as butterfly people each time something miraculous happened to save their lives!

One mother covered her three-year-old daughter as a car was hurtling toward them. The mother was astonished that nothing happened to them. The daughter then asked her mother, "Weren't they pretty? Didn't you see the butterfly people?" There are many other stories with the same theme, and only the children saw them. ("The Butterfly People of Joplin," Todd Frankel, *St. Louis Post Dispatch*, December 19, 2011)

Two cousins, Mason Lillard, age eleven, and Lage Grigsby, age fifteen, were in a truck that was thrown over 300 feet, and they sustained severe injuries. A rod went through Mason, and the cardiothoracic surgeon who saved her life said if it were one inch more either way, she wouldn't have made it. Lage was thought to be dying, so he was black-tagged and sent to the morgue. That same night, an ER nurse was reassigned to the morgue. While walking through, she accidentally touched Lage's arm, and he let out a scream. As a result, his life was saved. Mason said that right before the storm hit, she felt a touch on her shoulder. She turned and saw two angels in robes, which was calming. ("Cousins Recall Rescuing 'Angels' Rather Than Devastating Tornado," Susan Redden, *Joplin Globe*, May 21, 2016)

In downtown Joplin, we got to see a beautiful painting by award-winning muralist Dave Lowenstein, done with the help of 300 community volunteers. It is called "The Butterfly Effect: Dreams Take Flight." Also, to commemorate the fifth anniversary of the tornado, two butterfly sculptures were unveiled at Freeman Hospital and the Leffen Center for Autism.

This is one of several stories in this book where things happened after a prayer with odds that are off-the-charts. Some of the steps had laser-focused precision within seconds or minutes!

Becky made a prayerful appeal to find her childhood friend. Look at what it took.

- Group from Joplin (population 50,000) came to Las Vegas
- They chose Del Frisco's for dinner (6,000 restaurants in Las Vegas
- I was asked to take another sommelier's table

- They mentioned their city by name just as I arrived
- I called Becky about a party from Joplin (a first)
- They had the phone number of her friend

You might say, what's the big deal about reconnecting with a childhood friend compared to other dramatic miracles? That's the point It is a journey of great PERSONAL care!

LOVE IS the greatest and most powerful gift given to human beings. It is pure, unconditional, and never harms. Real love is demonstrated with action.

When my brother returned home and walked in to see our dad and said I love you, they fell on the floor weeping. That got me. It was completely different from my previous concepts and experiences of what love meant. That's when I knew something dramatic had happened to Michael, but he wouldn't tell me. It was the main reason I accepted his invitation to go to Los Angeles.

We had an ongoing rift between us from his birth until my life-changing experience. One night at about 3:00 a.m., I was sitting in a coffee shop with one of my new friends. Suddenly, the dam broke, and all this overwhelming love for my brother came pouring out. I was sobbing uncontrollably. It seemed like I went through a canister of napkins to wipe away all the tears. It was a new and remarkable freedom.

God is in the *Love* business!

CHAPTER 5

IT'S A HIGH CALLING

After my time as sommelier at the L'Escoffier, I worked five lunches and five to six dinner shifts as a server at Hy's Restaurant in the popular Century City area of Los Angeles near Beverly Hills. The job was very demanding, especially on busy nights with a lot of formal tableside service.

A LITTLE CARE, A BIG SURPRISE

One Thursday, Becky heard about a PGA golf tournament being held at Rancho Park, which was very close to work. She suggested I take a break between lunch and dinner shifts to go and watch the pros. After protesting because of being so tired, I decided to go. I was a pretty good golfer and had played on my high school team. When I got to the small chain-link fence at the 18th green, it was surprising that no fans were there. I was thrilled to see Arnold Palmer arrive very close to where I was standing. He glanced my way.

In addition to his excellent playing skills, his enormous popularity and infectious personality made him arguably golf's most outstanding ambassador. His nickname was "The King," and his many fans were referred to as Arnie's army. When I heard him talking to a fellow golfer, it was easy to understand that he was a very humble, genuine, down-to-earth human being who was so loved as a person, not just as a great golfer. When I got home that night, I thanked Becky so much for getting me to go and shared what I felt seeing him.

The next night, Hy's was packed. I approached one of my tables and saw Arnold Palmer sitting with Dow Finsterwald, another top pro. My jaw dropped, and I immediately sensed this was no accident. I mentioned to Arnie that I was the one person standing at the 18th green the day before.

Despite the challenge of taking care of many other customers, there was a peaceful calm. Everything at their table, as well as with my other customers, seemed to go smoothly. Although Arnie and Dow had an ongoing conversation, I felt a connection to Arnie. I wondered whether he was feeling anything similar. He laughed at a couple of my one-liner jokes. When they got up to leave, I was not at their table.

I saw him in the middle of the restaurant, and we both stopped about four feet from each other for more than the usual amount of time. He stared intensely into my eyes and tilted his head slowly to the left, then the right, continuing to stare. He walked slowly toward me, reached out to shake my hand, and in a very emphatic and deliberate tone said, "Thank you very much." Having waited on thousands of customers, including many celebrities and sports figures, nothing quite like that had ever happened. I was just a server in an apron, and he was one of the most iconic and legendary sports figures of all time. For me, it was as if there was something I was supposed to give him, but without words. It was a rare and humbling experience.

Out of my wife's care and concern for me working so much, and knowing how much I loved golf, she had suggested I take a break between shifts and go watch the golf. I hadn't wanted to make the effort, but the love for me that I heard in her voice made me realize I needed to go.

When Wine Is In Fashion

One afternoon at Del Frisco's, two men came in, one of whom introduced himself as Jeff Boisineau, a wine distributor. He, in turn, introduced Salvatore Ferragamo of IL Borro Winery in Tuscany, Italy. It is part of a beautiful medieval village restored by the Ferragamo family. That's when I learned that Salvatore, grandson of the iconic fashion family, had gone into the wine business and that two of his wines were on our list. (I had inherited the extensive list from the former sommelier and was unfamiliar with this winery.) We enjoyed a fun tasting, and the quality was outstanding. I assured them that I would be promoting the wines much more extensively.

Many years later, our son Jeremy was planning to visit Italy. It had been some time since I worked in the wine industry, and I hadn't been in touch with Salvatore for several years. I sent him an email, and within a few hours, he replied with a kind offer to meet Jeremy, which he so graciously did. Fast forward a few more years, where I am the sommelier at Albertsons Broadway in Boise, Idaho, a very upscale market with a chef, restaurant, and fine wine and food classes. I got in touch with the current IL Borro US representative, Francesco Peneider, who said he just happened to be in the process of trying to find a good Idaho distributor. We brought in their exceptional wine portfolio, and the customer feedback has been fantastic! The story of the Ferragamo name, outstanding organically grown wines, and showing photos of the incredible five-star estate has been an ongoing success.

The first meeting started as a business relationship, but it has evolved into a friendship. In October 2019, Becky and I were privileged and honored to be invited guests at the magnificent Tuscany property. You never know who you're going to meet in the hospitality industry.

A FIRST LADY'S SONG

One night in the early 1980s, the back section of L'Escoffier was reserved for a private party of sixteen. The guest of honor was Mrs. Imelda Marcos, then First Lady of the Philippines. At that time, she was arguably the most popular female leader in the world. To most, she is famous for her collection of more than a thousand pairs of shoes.

The host was Dr. Armand Hammer, CEO of Occidental Petroleum. As a medical doctor and philanthropist supporting education, the arts, and medicine, he had received numerous worldwide honors. So, sitting there was a party with two of the most highly influential people in the world.

A bodyguard was seated at a separate table on each end of the party. As I approached, I was pleasantly surprised to hear Mrs. Marcos singing the popular song "Feelings," and with such a pretty voice. It was fortuitous that the cashier for that evening was Bayani, a fine Filipino man. The cashier's station was out of the view of customers, and when I told him that Madam Marcos was a guest, he couldn't believe it.

I am good with languages and asked Bayani if he would quickly teach me how to say "you sang beautifully" in Tagalog (*ang ganda mong kumanta*), the native language of the Philippines. Although I knew him to be very gracious, I nervously and jokingly added to please not mess around and have me say something inappropriate. He laughed, and I felt fine. After a bit of rehearsal, he assured me I would be well understood.

I walked around the table serving Dom Perignon champagne, and as I poured Madam Marcos her glass, I said to her in perfect

Tagalog that she sang beautifully. She immediately grabbed my hand and turned around to face me. Then came a collective gasp, and I looked up to see everyone holding their breath with jaws dropped.

When I saw the two bodyguards reaching into their holsters for their guns, I understood that everyone might have thought I had threatened her. Although I was not trained for this type of situation, my immediate reaction was to smile and keep calm. In that moment of high tension, with one of her hands holding mine and the other hand over her heart, the first lady turned back around to her guests and said that I had just told her in her native language that she sang beautifully.

Everyone, including me, breathed a huge sigh of relief, and the bodyguards took their hands off the guns. Dr. Hammer gave me a look that I could only interpret as, okay kid, that was bold and audacious. Mrs. Marcos returned for dinner a few nights later, and she came over and gave me a big thank you hug!

When I heard Mrs. Marcos sing, I wanted to let her know it was beautiful. I tried to think of what I could do that might be a nice personal touch and bring her a smile. It dawned upon me that we had a Filipino cashier on duty. I could never have imagined what happened. How did little ole me touch the heart of one of the most influential people in the world?

CHAPTER 6

CARE AND RESPECT

Life is all about relationships. When you're on the job eight hours a day, five days a week, you have close relationships with your associates. Of course, you want to do a good job for the boss and take good care of the customers and any staff for whom you are responsible. But what about other associates and suppliers who provide much needed services and products? Do you treat them with the same respect? It's the difference between what's in it for me and what I can do to uplift someone else. When you treat everyone with the same care, it can produce rewards for you and them.

UNEXPECTED HELP

After a late-night restaurant shift as a server in Hy's Restaurant, my car wouldn't start. I needed a ride home. Who offered with much enthusiasm? A busboy, and it was far out of his way. I asked him why he offered. He said it was because I treated the busboys with the same respect as everyone else, including making them laugh, and he was grateful. It's the little things that mean so much.

I had many chats with one of the busboys at Del Frisco's. He was a terrific, hardworking young man, about the same age as my son. He made his goals known to management that he wanted the opportunity to be promoted to server or sommelier and was told he would get his chance. Some time went by with no promotion, and he trusted me enough to share that he was going to quit. Can anyone relate to getting impatient? That affected me because I believed his promotion was coming, and I appealed to him to stay. He changed his mind, got promoted to sommelier, and earned good money for someone still in college. He later thanked me for the encouragement I had given him. It is a great joy and reward to help others.

AN ISLAND ADVENTURE

At Del Frisco's, I was both head sommelier and assistant manager. I usually closed the restaurant three nights a week. When the general manager wasn't there, I was in charge of the entire large staff. I loved to encourage and uplift them and make them laugh. It was a two-way street, and they provided so many beautiful moments for me. The relationship with fellow workers is of great importance.

My Del Frisco's job came while I was working in sales for a wine distributor. I kept both jobs for some time until it was too much. One day, I was out in the field seeing wine accounts with John Bookwalter, owner of the outstanding Bookwalter Winery in Richland, Washington. John shared so much about Washington that I thought it might be nice to visit. My wife and I were trying to figure out a family vacation at that time. After the sales day, I went to work at Del Frisco's, and of the several hostesses working that evening, I was greeted at the front by Sarah who asked how my day was going. When I shared about my Washington adventure, she told me she was from Seattle. Hmmm, Washington twice within the hour. So, I asked her advice about vacation ideas. I wasn't expecting what came next. She wondered if I'd be interested in taking my family to Whidbey Island off the coast of Washington, where her friend, on active duty in Iraq, had a home with an award-winning view of the water. She explained it was a beautiful setting and that the way you get there is to fly into Seattle, rent a car, and drive onto a ferry. Offering to call him and ask if we could stay at his house, I was blown away and gave her an immediate yes. A few days later, she confirmed we could stay in his home as a gift to us. Wow!

It was a fantastic time for our family. The scenery was magnificent, and the water views of the sunsets at 10:00 p.m. were breathtaking. The ferry rides, picking berries, and endless outdoor activities were so much fun. The highlight had to be a whale-watching cruise from Orcas Island in the San Juan Islands. We drove to the town of Anacortes over a beautiful bridge high above the river. It was a picture-postcard view. At Anacortes, we took the ferry to Orcas Island and boarded our boat. The captain told us we were fortunate to be there on one of the two or three days a year when three pods of whales converged in one area. Some came close to the boat, jumping and flipping as if they wanted to entertain us. What an extraordinary time! When you encourage and uplift others, it sometimes brings surprises.

AFTER FIVE YEARS at Del Frisco's, I said my goodbyes to the staff. Everyone had such an emotional response that Becky and I decided to have a going-away party at our house. What a great turnout. Becky had met some of the staff on different occasions, and others she met that day for the first time. The amount of love, gratitude, and tears that everyone expressed to Becky about me was humbling and overwhelming. Having care and respect for others is a veritable treasure in life.

CHAPTER 7

JOB CHALLENGES OR OPPORTUNITIES?

My sales and management career in various industries includes hospitality in restaurant food and wine service. Although that covers a lot, this book relates to ALL work situations. I share what I learned about the best way to see and treat customers, the boss, and fellow employees.

Here's where the rubber meets the road. Almost everyone is fine when things are going well. How do you handle the problems when they come? And they do, don't they? Getting past challenging situations starts with being calm, not taking it personally, and believing there is a way through. In addition to some pearls, you may find these stories entertaining.

A study published a few years ago found that being a restaurant server may be more stressful than was previously realized, even more so than being a doctor, teacher, scientist, etc.[1] Another report showed that the hotel, food services, and hospitality industries had the highest burnout rate in the world.[2] Take it for what it's worth. My poor wife. I include this to show what this book is about and what really works.

With that in mind, there is great value in having high self-esteem. If you base your self-esteem on your position, achievements, material possessions, earnings, relationships, etc., it can go up and down like a roller coaster. Down it goes if someone else gets promoted to a position you felt you deserved. When you're doing pretty well, some other people are always doing better. It never ends, and that can be very discouraging. It's like building a house on a sand foundation. When the storms come, it falls down.

There's good news! When I had my life-changing experience, I became aware that I was loved and esteemed. It had nothing to do with anything good I had ever done. When you know that you know, you are not easily shaken. That means when the challenges of life come, you're on solid rock with boldness, confidence, and freedom to do extraordinary things.

CHANGING LIABILITIES TO ASSETS

Hy's Steak House was a big, opulent, two-level restaurant situated in the middle of many tall office buildings filled with highly successful attorneys and other business professionals. While in the kitchen on a particular evening, I heard one server after another, followed by the chefs, just start cursing. As I stood there wondering what was going on, several of them, in one accord, turned around, pointed at me, and started laughing. They said, "Stephen can take care of them." "Take care of who?" I asked. That night was a reservation for a successful accountant and his wife who came in for dinner every few weeks and had a routine that drove everyone crazy through obligation and manipulation. No one wanted to wait on them. The staff said that if anyone could handle them, it was me. I couldn't resist hearing their story.

I was told the couple would always come in and order an appetizer to share, including an expensive item like smoked salmon. They would insist on getting a much larger portion at no extra charge. They would bring in their own tea bags, and the server was required to bring boiling hot water in cups numerous times during the meal. No matter how hot it was, it was never hot enough, so you'd have to go back and do it again and again. Then came the entrée that they also shared. No matter what vegetables or starch were served with the dinner, it wasn't good enough. They insisted on getting what they wanted, and if the chef didn't have it, they asked if he could go to the store while they waited. The entrée had to be so hot that the server would hold it with three towels. They would take one bite, say it's too cold, send it back, and insist it had to be thrown out and a fresh dish prepared. And at the end of the meal, they would leave a very small tip!

My immediate reaction was that it was both funny and sad. I decided to accept the challenge and was determined to do anything I could to change the situation. My plan was to shower them with kindness, humor, charm, and sacrifice, and not to be at all focused on everything they were going to throw at me. My first goal for a successful milestone was to get them not to turn back their entrée, which was a personal offense to the chefs and cost the restaurant money. I started with a warm smile and conveyed that I was looking forward to meeting them. Game on! Although everything went just as explained, I kept a very upbeat attitude as I got them extra food and the particular vegetables requested. The hard part was convincing the chefs to go along with me and go out of their way. I didn't make them any promises, and they reluctantly agreed. With every special thing done in the kitchen, I communicated to the guests that the team wanted to provide a good experience. When it was time to serve the entrée, I stood by as the chef heated the plate to an outrageous temperature. I grabbed it and ran right out to the table to ensure it was very, very hot and explained that it was. I walked away and came back one minute later, expecting to see smiling faces, only to hear, "Please take it back, it's too cold!" Although I was hoping that wouldn't happen, I was prepared and kept to the plan of being cheerful. The chef didn't take it so well, but I assured him and the staff that I wouldn't give up.

I must have made some progress because the next time in, they requested me as their server. The routine was the same, the results were the same, and the entrée got sent back. The third time was a charm. I did even more than the extras they were asking for, all the while maintaining being happy. I responded to their behavior with so much attention that a breakthrough finally came. I approached the table with the usual, "How is your dinner?" When they said it was wonderful and didn't send it back, I was elated and noticed a dramatic change in their demeanor. Their usual whiny, sheepish behavior immediately turned into a happy, outgoing couple who looked ten years younger. It was fascinating. And that night was the first time they left a 20% tip.

The next time in, they brought pictures of their kids and grandkids and were completely different people. They wanted to meet the chefs, and when I brought them out from the kitchen, the cursing and anger turned to hugs, joy, and reconciliation. By that time, the rest of the staff had heard what happened, and the other servers wanted to wait on them upon return visits. It was fine with me that everyone wanted to spread a little love around to our "new guests."

You might ask, why go through all that for less money in a job with enough stress? Great question, and my answer is why not? Care is often measured in terms of sacrifice. No matter what happened, I would not let it affect me. Since the challenge was thrown at me, I thought it would be great if I could do anything (there was no way to know) that could help a couple come out of their problem. It all worked out well, and my reward was to see a fine couple get released and come out of their shell to enjoy life. How about what it might mean to their family, friends, and community, not to mention all the restaurant workers?

Back Room To Front Page

Even the most inglorious, demeaning, nitty-gritty job situations can have some happy and surprising results. Although I was very excited to get my first head sommelier job at L'Escoffier, I quickly learned that I inherited a real mess. The wines had been numbered to match the wine list, but they were stored all over the place and hard to find. I could only imagine it was a form of job security for the prior sommelier, since it would be hard for anyone else to find the wines. The wine coolers and racks looked like dirt and grease had built up for years. Yuck! What to do? This had to be taken care of, and I figured I was the guy who needed to do it. I approached the restaurant manager to explain the situation, offering to organize the wines and do a major cleanup. He was very supportive of the project. I estimated it would take me three days to do everything; however, he could only get hotel management to commit to one extra day's pay. That meant working two days without pay to clean up the mess, which was totally against my old, spoiled nature. I decided to do it anyway, choosing gratitude for the job and respect for my department over logic.

On one of the three days, I was alone for fourteen hours over a July 4th weekend. I vividly remember asking myself, "What the heck am I doing? Does anyone even know what is involved? Does anyone care?" But I pressed through, realizing what a great job opportunity I had. Why not show some care and appreciation? It would be so much better for the whole staff.

A short time later, Margy Rochlin, a reporter for the prestigious *LA Magazine*, contacted me to request an interview including photographs as part of an article, "Eight Great Jobs." She explained that they felt the sommelier of a world-class Beverly Hills restaurant, who sampled wines in his tastevin, serving high-profile customers and leaders from all over the world, would be perfect for their article. She also told me the photos would be taken in the wine cellar (which I had just finished cleaning up). Well, that was unexpected!

Initially, I turned down the offer. I know that seems crazy, but I was also involved in selling a research medical device for children's heart surgery, and I didn't think it wise to get labeled in the restaurant business (foolish pride). When it was pointed out that I should be thinking of how this would benefit my employer, the light went on. My thinking went from self-centered to my employer. I then got very excited, called to accept the interview, and was happy to learn the opportunity still existed.

The reporter and photographer would have to go through the wine cooler area, cashier station, and service bar to get to the wine cellar. These areas were out of customer view and hadn't been painted in ages. But since my focus was on presenting the best possible image for the hotel, I decided the areas needed a facelift. That meant wall décor as well as painting. The restaurant staff laughed at me, saying they had been trying to get those things done for years, and they were sure nothing was going to change.

That didn't discourage me one bit because I believed a nice appearance would make a good impression on local media members. Their mockery probably added a little incentive. When I asked the maintenance department to get the project done, they laughed it off. I kept pleading my case, and, finally, they agreed to do it. I just smiled when I saw the disbelief on staff faces as the work began. The changes made the atmosphere more enjoyable for them too. In a small way, I hoped it would encourage all of them to pursue the courage of their convictions.

Before Margy and the photographer arrived, I arranged with the head chef to prepare some hors d'oeuvres. At that time, I was not thinking much about the interview but rather about giving them a wonderful time. It all went great, and they loved everything, the wine, the food, and even my ongoing jokes. A few weeks later, Margy called to let me know they had such a good time that they were putting my interview and picture first in the article! I was both honored and humbled by the entire experience.

California restaurant writers would dine at L'Escoffier from time to time. When they asked to see the wine cellar, I was happy to show it. Not long after, the California Restaurant Writers Association awarded me Sommelier of the Year! I had no idea that was coming. I'm glad the area was presentable.

Did I have to clean up someone's mess without being paid for most of the work? No! The feeling of quitting came up. Can anyone relate? Did I have to spend my energy with hotel management to get the unseen areas painted? No! Then why? Life is not always a scorecard. It was great to be able to do something that I would not have even considered in the past. The rewards were more than expected.

It took commitment to finish the job when all the emotions to quit came up. It was a good reminder that you're never alone, and everything you do for the right reasons is noticed. That is comforting.

Pride or Passion?

Being passionate about your work is another quality we all know to be valuable. Most people can be passionate when they are doing things they love. Fair enough. So, here's the question. Can you be passionate and upbeat about something that may not be so exciting to you? After six years of being a sommelier in the Beverly Hills and Los Angeles area, my next job was as a server at a seafood restaurant close to where I lived. Although it was a nice restaurant, it was a far cry from my previous job, earnings, and atmosphere. Larry Lipson, author and restaurant writer, came in for lunch one day. He was part of the California Restaurant Writers Association that presented me with the Sommelier of the

Year award at L'Escoffier. As soon as I saw him, I felt embarrassed about where I was working compared to where he last saw me. As his server, I had to decide quickly. Would I stay in my pride or shake it off so I could give him my best? During a brief discussion of our lunch special, I animatedly described the dish I thought he would enjoy. He became very excited and told me about his radio program called *The Wine Cellar*. He asked if I would be the guest speaker for his upcoming "Excellent Restaurant Service" episode. I certainly wasn't expecting that but immediately accepted the invitation. On the air, Larry gave me great respect and honor during the interview and questions from the audience.

Looking back, it is interesting that I was invited as a server and NOT as Sommelier of the Year. It was passion in the humbler job that moved him! When Larry came in, I recognized my prideful reaction and turned right back to the land of the living. It was a definite choice that made the difference. Introduction by Larry on the air: "Stephen's enthusiasm and passion are what restaurant service is all about." (Larry Lipson, Restaurant Critic, Author, Host KGIL Radio, Los Angeles, California: *The Wine Cellar*)

VALUE OF VALUES

One of the most challenging moments on a job came when my boss asked me to do something against my values. Until then, we had a great relationship. I was the sommelier when a large party ordered around twenty-five bottles of one of the least expensive wines on the list. The boss's spouse had come by for a visit, and I was asked to put an extra bottle of wine on the customer's check so the boss and spouse could enjoy wine with their dinner. I had never refused anything I was asked to do up to that point and had a pit in my stomach when I said I couldn't do that. The boss got upset with me for the first and only time and told me I'd be fired if I refused. It was a good job, and I was distraught. Earlier, the party host had told me not to save the empty wine bottles because he trusted the amount would be correct. In other words, no one would know. Then came the rationalization that it is not my doing if I'm only obeying orders. That was followed by thinking if it is such a small dollar amount, it wouldn't matter.

Despite all those thoughts, I still couldn't say yes. As I walked through the restaurant feeling very discouraged, I looked up and said, "Great, I'm trying to do the right thing, and I'm about to lose a good job!" The next thing I heard was the voice of the manager's spouse calling me over. Was this going to be like the scene in *It's a Wonderful Life* when Jimmy Stewart asks God for help and then gets punched? I figured a lecture might come on what an idiot I was for refusing such a simple request. What happened was a shock. I was told the spouse knew what happened between the boss and me, and they assured me that I wouldn't get fired. What a huge relief. Then I was told how fortunate the boss was to have someone like me working there and how proud they were that I stood up for my values. Yes, tears welled up in my eyes, and my relationship with the boss after the incident was better than ever.

When your values are tested, it can be a tough decision. When the boss asked me to add a bottle of wine to a customer's check, it was a challenging test because I had choices. I almost wish I could have just said yes. Something I didn't think of at the time might have been the better way to go. I could have genuinely offered that, although I couldn't do what he asked, I would be happy to buy the boss a bottle of wine, even a better one. Thank God for a good ending! Whew!

SURVIVOR'S GUILT RELEASED

At L'Escoffier, the head cashier was an outspoken Jewish woman who had been living in Germany when Hitler came into power. At age seventeen, she was on her way home from school when someone she trusted got hold of her and told her she had to leave the country immediately. She believed them and fled.

During many conversations with her, she shared her enormous grief, guilt, and anger as she recalled the atrocities saying, "Why was I spared?" and, "How could God let that happen?" One day, I was sitting on the floor putting away wines right below the counter where she was. The two of us were conversing, but there was no eye contact. With no apparent provocation, she began shrieking and screaming at me. I felt my bones rattle. Then a clear thought came to me that she was really mad at God and not me. It wasn't anything personal. I further understood she trusted the care I had for her because I wouldn't judge her or fight back.

Dealing with atrocities or tragedies can be highly emotional and painful. In most cases, the memories never go away. It takes courage to bare your heart in front of another person, and I wanted to be compassionate and respectful at a very sensitive moment. A little while later, she calmed down, and I was glad for her sake that nobody else was around.

When she came in the next day, I greeted her in my usual friendly manner as if nothing had happened. She had a beaming smile that I hadn't seen on her before, and she looked ten to fifteen years younger. I excitedly told her how good she looked and asked what was happening. She explained she'd had very high blood pressure for a long time and had gone to the doctor for a checkup earlier that day. With a proud, huge smile, she said the doctor reported that her blood pressure had gone down to the level of a healthy young woman for the first time in a long time. She was thrilled, and so was I!

It is a mysterious phenomenon. When we throw our grief and anger at God, we can be healed! Looking back, an essential part of the story was that I did not confront her. Instead, I just let her get it all out. I had no idea what was to follow.

Last Laugh

Let's lighten it up. A good sense of humor can change situations. Mine is always spontaneous, with no clue what will come out of my mouth. It's often zany or outrageous, which sometimes makes my wife cringe. She is concerned that some people may take me seriously.

Del Frisco's Steak House in Las Vegas has a wine cellar private dining room with wood-paneled walls, stone floors, and ceiling-to-floor windows looking into the temperature-controlled wine bins. It's an excellent atmosphere for wine lovers. One night, a party of sixteen arrived, and the host explained that they were a wine club that flew in from Los Angeles.

The dinner was their annual food and wine event. They were to select the wines for the first two courses and asked if I would choose the wine for the entrée. The budget was at least $300 per bottle and could be $400 to $500, but it had to be very, very good. The host then added that they would be talking about whatever wine I chose for some time. The pressure was on. To make it more enjoyable, I suggested brown bagging the wine, which meant hiding the bottle. He thought that was a great idea that would allow everyone to guess what it was.

One of the guests started pounding on the table with boisterous laughter, saying, "Bring on the Gallo swill." It was an obvious mockery about Gallo's low-priced table wines, and everyone looked embarrassed by his behavior. At that moment, the light went on, and I knew exactly what wine I would choose. Most people are not aware that Gallo has some outstanding single-vineyard wines. Their estate red wines are among the top in California. I chose Gallo Estate 1994 Cabernet Sauvignon, poured the wine into crystal decanters, and brought the actual bottles in brown bags. I poured a taste for the host and was thrilled when he turned around to all his guests and said it was even better than he had hoped. He assumed I had selected a $500 bottle to get that quality level. The "Gallo man" made another boisterous, sarcastic comment. Then when he took his first taste, he spoke out and said, "Ooh, ooh, I've got it. It is either Phelps Insignia or Silver Oak, Napa Valley." I loved his reaction because he guessed two of California's most prestigious and iconic wines. Others were discussing their ideas of what they were drinking.

When it came time to unveil the mystery wine, everyone looked curiously at the two other sommeliers and a manager I brought into the room. I said, "You are all wondering why everyone is here, and the reason is that you are enjoying a Gallo Estate wine!" They cheered and went into hysterics. When the man who had mocked Gallo threw his head down on the table and said, "See, I told you," everyone laughed even harder. The host was very pleased when I told him the price was below the low end of their budget. Watch what you say. The last laugh might be on you.

MAKE 'EM LAUGH

Over several months, Larry Smith, Manager of the Chaparral Restaurant at Camelback Inn, Scottsdale, Arizona, prepared me for the arrival of a VIP guest from Wyoming. During past visits, he had made everyone a nervous wreck. Larry pleaded with me to take care of this guest because he had great confidence in my humor and ability to handle difficult and demanding customers.

It would have been well within my position to tell Larry that he was the manager, and I was just the host. I thought the whole scenario was amusing, and, of course, I told him I would do my thing. Actually, I couldn't wait to meet the VIP. Every week I'd get a reminder of the guest's arrival date. Each time I'd give my assurance that I was ready. When the day came, I was at the front podium when Larry let me know he was there. I spontaneously rushed to the front door and gave him a warm, open-hearted greeting. "I'm Stephen. I've heard so much about you and couldn't wait to meet you!" When I saw a stunned look on his face, it seemed things were off to a good start. I found him to be very gracious and personable.

He was an affluent businessman. One evening he came in with a group for dinner, and I asked how he was doing. He said things were rough, and he wasn't sure he could afford to fly home. That's when I realized he had a good sense of humor. It was show time. I was aware that his dinner party of six included the CEO of a prestigious bank in world-renowned Jackson Hole, Wyoming. I couldn't resist and immediately took his arm and walked him to his table. I said to everyone, "Excuse me, your associate is concerned about having enough money to return home. I'm here to take up a collection to help him out." They all cheered and cracked up laughing. He slapped me on the back, stuck some money in my pocket, and said that was great.

The VIP and all his guests had a fantastic time. There were no problems for Larry. A few weeks later, I got a handwritten letter of invitation to visit Jackson Hole and that we would be personally taken care of by them. He had just wanted to have a good time. Why not take on a challenge? Humor can go a long way.

Whoops!

How do you respond when a customer appears to be having issues? Leslie Nielsen, the famous actor and comedian, was sitting with a party of six at one of my tables. As I passed by where he was seated, I heard a sound come from him that, let's say, could be embarrassing. I did my best to pretend I didn't hear it and noticed the people at the table were doing the same.

A few minutes later, it happened again. Then I looked more closely at the other guests. They were desperately trying to maintain not breaking into hysterics. That's when I got it. He had a whoopee cushion, and everyone wanted to see how I would deal with it. I cracked up.

Almost everyone, including myself, enjoys being around people with a good sense of humor to lift spirits. I enjoy being that person.

UNCORKED

What about the times when we cause the problem and just have to do the best we can? It was lunchtime in the beautiful, wood-paneled Bernard's restaurant in the famous downtown LA Biltmore Hotel. The room, with incredible acoustics, was unusually quiet as I greeted a table of six older ladies. They ordered champagne to start things off. I had gotten a little behind and briskly walked to grab the bottle and get to the table. In my haste, I didn't take the time to notice that the bottle was not chilled and inadvertently shook the bottle.

When I removed the wiring, I heard the loudest explosion ever from a cork! It took off like a rocket, and the very expensive crystal chandelier pieces above the table rattled. I was terrified to look up and assess the damage. My thoughts were that this was the end of my job, and it could take years to pay for the repairs.

I gathered myself to look down at the ladies, and it wasn't a pretty sight. Five of them were grabbing onto the tablecloth with pale faces. The sixth lady was under the table and stuck her head out to ask if the shooter was still there. While I was concerned about a broken chandelier, the ladies believed a gunman was in the room! After extending a huge apology, I quickly explained that it was the champagne cork. Then I profusely offered ongoing calming reassurance and did everything possible to give them the most attentive and caring service.

When you cause the problem, start with being humble and apologetic. Being defensive, feeling guilty, or deflecting blame will only worsen things. And remember, don't open warm or shaken champagne!

WALK-A-BYE

Sometimes it's something simple and practical. On one occasion at Bernard's, a mom became uncomfortable because her baby was very restless. She didn't know what to do. That's always a challenge for the service team. Although I was just the sommelier, the thought came to me to offer to take the baby for a little walk around the restaurant. It seemed unrealistic since I was a stranger. The thought persisted, so I decided to ask and check it out. I told her I was a dad and that if it would help, I'd walk the baby for a bit. To my surprise, she said yes. A few minutes later, I came back, and the baby was as calm as could be. The mom was thrilled, and I was pleasantly surprised. No, I'm not available for babysitting services. Thank you, though.

GOOD CHOICES TO CONSIDER:

- **Enjoy what you are doing even if you don't like the situation.**

Being happy does not have to depend on circumstances. After bringing my team to number one in the country, the company I worked for had financial struggles. I wound up as a maître d' in my lowest paying job ever. I wasn't thrilled; however, I didn't let the circumstances change the way I did things.

Little supervision was needed because Stephen was always reliable and showed initiative to take on additional assignments. He developed and implemented Camelback Inn's first and very successful wine training program, with wine and food tasting seminars. Sales in the restaurant and resort rose by twenty percent. In 1996, we were named Hotel of the Year. It is my strong belief that Stephen contributed in obtaining these honors. (Excerpts from a letter of recommendation from Larry Smith, Restaurant Operations Manager)

Stephen is a role model when displaying genuine and enthusiastic interest in the guest. He truly wants to make the guest experience unforgettable. (Job Performance Review, Marriott's Camelback Inn (5-Star/5-Diamond), Scottsdale, Arizona, Larry Smith, Manager)

- **Don't judge.**

This is huge in all areas of life, especially in service and hospitality. It simply means you don't condemn, criticize, or get upset with anyone, regardless of their behavior. Use good judgment to see how you can contribute to making a situation better. We have no idea what other people are going through and how much a little care and kindness could mean to them in difficult times. Besides being your job, having compassion instead of judgment can dramatically change your life.

~

Sales And Sales Management

The restaurant at the Camelback Inn in Scottsdale, Arizona, closed for an extended time to remodel. So, my wife and I decided to take on a new adventure and moved our family to our first small town, Bishop, California, where we had a few good friends. I was hired by Wine Warehouse, a premier wine distributor with an outstanding portfolio. It was a commission-only independent rep job, and I thought if I could significantly grow the business, they may put me on salary, commissions, and expenses. Other reps from different distributors had been servicing the customers for some time. What could I do differently? First, I took time to learn what the needs and wants of the people were. It was quite different from big-city thinking. Then I convinced the local market owner to allow me to form a wine club. He liked my ideas, and so it began. I successfully got many personable suppliers to come to the region to put on events in Bishop and the Mammoth Mountain Ski Area. I also arranged for them to do wine tastings at different restaurants. In addition, I wrote articles for the local newspaper promoting the happenings. Several charities and foundations had me participate in their fundraising events. All these things were new to me and turned out to be exceptionally well received. My sales doubled, and I was hired as a full-time employee.

Here are some recognitions:

> *Stephen daily went above and beyond in his customer service. It was apparent that wine was more than a job for him. It was PASSION.*
>
> — Irv Wnuck, Sr. Vice President (Retired), Wine Warehouse

> *What Stephen did was truly amazing... in forming a wine appreciation/tasting club for the region, and in doing so, is responsible for educating the region to an unbelievable level and awareness.*

> — KIT NAGELMANN, BRAND MANAGER, LABOURE-ROI BURGUNDY/DUBOS FRERE BORDEAUX

> *I have observed him taking over the market in his region through his efforts in organizing wine clubs, winemaker dinners, as well as newspaper columns. Both events I did with him were sellouts and first-class.*

> — DAVID MIRASSOU, SIXTH GENERATION OF THE OLDEST WINE FAMILY IN THE US

> *Mr. Walker has been instrumental in helping my wine department grow and expand into other areas, thus benefiting my whole store.*

> — KYLE ONEY, OWNER, MANOR MARKET, RETAIL SUPERMARKET

> *Stephen is a definite out-of-the-box thinker.*

> — MICHELE KESTER, BRAND MANAGER, WINE QUEST

Stephen's enthusiasm and creativity have produced several new ideas that have been a valuable contribution to our restaurant.

— Frederic Pierrel, Executive Chef, Lakefront Restaurant, Mammoth Lakes

Stephen Walker has been an invaluable asset as a volunteer soliciting donations for this lucrative event ... Stephen has been a pleasure to work with and extremely productive in his different capacities.

— Evan Russell, President and CEO, Mammoth Lakes Foundation (College), Charitable

Stephen has been a great asset. He demonstrates ... reliability, creativity, enthusiasm, and the ability to meet deadlines.

— Bernice de la Salle, Interim Director, Mono County Arts Council, Charitable

CHAPTER 8

IT'S NOT ALWAYS LOGICAL

We all respond to situations through our combined experience, personality, and how we do things. That makes logical sense.

But a whole other world is going on all around us. There was a time I actually had a brick wall built over my bedroom window, had three locks on the door, and no doorbell. I didn't want to hear or see anything. It is just the opposite now. Often, a new idea or impression to do something that makes no sense comes up. I am curious to explore where it is coming from in those situations. If it seemed like the right kind of knock, and I responded, amazing things happened.

LIVE LIFE TO WIN THE RACE

In November 2002, legendary race car driver Mario Andretti came into Del Frisco's for dinner with a small group. He also owns Andretti Winery in Napa, California. Since two of his wines were on our list, I had the opportunity to have a brief conversation with him. Immediately, I sensed his humility and fineness, and I added an extra behind-the-scenes personal touch to the dinner service. A few days later, I got a letter from him saying how much he enjoyed the dining experience, with his sincerest thanks for my hospitality. It was signed, "Your Friend, Mario Andretti." He said he'd come back to Del Frisco's when in Las Vegas, and he did.

Fast forward a few years. One day out of the blue, I had a strong impression that I should go to the next Indy 500 race and take my son. Logically, I didn't understand it since I'd never been to a car race. And his behavior at the time was such that it wasn't something I would have even considered doing. It was fascinating as I realized two sides of me were having a conversation with opposing views. I dismissed the idea.

A few weeks later, the same experience came up again, and I decided to run it by Becky, who I was sure would just tell me to let it go. She surprised me by saying that maybe such a crazy idea would be a catalyst to motivate Jeremy. So, the decision to go was made. The next unexpected surprise was that he said yes to the trip.

A few months before the race, Mario came back to Del Frisco's, and I rushed over to him with great enthusiasm to tell him that my son and I would be going to our first Indy 500. To my absolute shock, he gave me his cell number to call him when we arrived. I decided not to say anything to Jeremy in case we didn't meet him.

I planned a three-day weekend for the Sunday, May 29th, 2005, race. I took Jeremy out to dinner on Friday evening and sneaked outside to call Mario. He answered and told me we should meet him at his hotel the next day. It revved me up (pun intended). I kept it a secret and was biting my lip as we sat in the hotel lobby while Jeremy was grumbling about what we were doing there. When Mario came in, Jeremy's jaw dropped! Mario told us to jump into his car, and he took us to the Andretti Green Racing Team Garage, run by his son Michael. It was the day before the race, and we had a fabulous behind-the-scenes tour.

I took several photos with Mario and Jeremy of cars whose drivers turned out to be future Indy 500 winners, like Dario Franchitti and Tony Kanaan. I asked Mario if he could arrange just one picture with the three of us, which turned out to be the one in front of the Red and White #26 car to be driven the next day by Dan Wheldon. That evening in our hotel room, I stood next to Jeremy, thanked God for Mario's hospitality, and asked a blessing on him for the kindness he had shown to us. To our amazement, Dan Wheldon won the race!

My son Jeremy and me with Mario Andretti the day before the 2005 Indy 500. Mario gave us a private tour in the Andretti Garage. The car pictured was driven on race day by Dan Wheldon who won!

I would like to think that the invitation to the Indy 500 several months earlier was an inspiration and encouragement to help Jeremy complete his regular school courses as well as some online classes he was behind in. That would allow him to graduate on time with his senior class. And he did so with good grades. As parents, we often don't know what is needed for our kids. Leadings may come that make no logical sense.

Okay, we all get new thoughts from time to time. In this case, there was no doubt in my mind that it wasn't coming from me because I was debating within myself. It had to be a discernment. Please allow me to laugh out loud at myself for dismissing it so quickly. Fortunately, it came back a second time, and Becky to the rescue.

Not Always About You

In 2003, we were refinancing our mortgage when we discovered that the lender had deceptively slipped in a pre-payment penalty clause after agreeing to not have one. I made many phone calls over several months and kept running into a brick wall (there's that wall again). One day in a moment of frustration, I mumbled that, if necessary, I would call the Attorney General of the United States to resolve this mortgage issue. It seemed ridiculous to have such a thought, and I laughed at the absurdity of it all.

That night, a local Las Vegas attorney brought a dinner party into Del Frisco's. We'd only met a few times, and I was taken aback when he introduced me to his guests as a top sommelier. They were dignitaries from Washington, DC, including an Energy Commission head. I recalled my earlier thoughts in the day about then Attorney General John Ashcroft, and I stood speechless, thinking she would surely know him. It took a few minutes to process that this might not be a coincidence. Then, in a heightened state of excitement, I realized this had nothing to do with my silly mortgage battle (which eventually got resolved). Instead, my thoughts went to my father-in-law, Bob J. Vernon, who grew up in Missouri and had lived in Springfield, where John is from. Bob had composed two patriotic songs, "Tell America" and "Freedom Prayer," which were part of his Capitol Records album, *The Inspiration of Bob Vernon*, recorded with the famed arranger Ralph Carmichael.

He had previously told me that John Ashcroft contacted him in the 1960s after hearing these two songs on the radio and asked about getting the sheet music. Bob gave him permission to sing the songs and had always wanted to get back in touch with an updated CD. So, I rushed to the phone, and Bob told me to absolutely feel free to ask if the Commissioner could get the CD to him along with some photos. She said she would be happy to and gave me her contact information. Both Bob and I received very cordial thank-you letters from Attorney General Ashcroft, who said he looked forward to playing and listening to the music again.

As a WWII Navy submarine veteran, Bob was inspired to write these patriotic songs during the Vietnam War, which led to a USO singing tour in Vietnam arranged by the United States Department of Defense for Bob and his teenage daughter Becky (now my cute wife). When they returned, Becky's high school superintendent arranged an assembly to honor the Vernons' trip, but Bob had a previously planned event in South Africa and could not attend. So, Becky, dressed in Army fatigues covered in badges and pins from the units visited in Vietnam, was the star.

It was outrageous and laughable for me to think of contacting the United States Attorney General to help with a bank dispute. Are you kidding? Sometimes thoughts have a different purpose than what you were initially thinking.

Chardonnay Saves The Day

One evening, a man came into L'Escoffier and was seated at a window table with a view from Beverly Hills to downtown Los

Angeles. He asked me to choose a fine chardonnay from California or France. I brought him an exceptional white Burgundy (French Chardonnay). He was delighted. Soon after, a couple was seated at the table beside him. Strangely, they also asked me to choose a chardonnay from either California or France. For them, I selected a good one from California. It was quite unusual for the same request to come from two parties, let alone at tables next to each other. Then a thought came to me that I never had before. I told the man about the couple making the same wine request and asked him if he would be interested in trading wine tastes with them. He loved the idea, as did the couple.

A few minutes after their toast, the man asked me what they had ordered for dinner. I told him it was a beef dish. He then said to bring them a bottle of Chateau Lafite Rothschild and put it on his check. That is one of the world's finest and most expensive red wines. After gathering my composure, I told the couple about the very generous offer. They were thrilled and explained it was their 25th Anniversary. They had planned the evening for months, including putting aside a little money from their modest budget. I shared their response with the man, and the three of them sat down for a brief visit before their dinners arrived.

I was trying to figure out why someone would buy such an expensive wine for two strangers. The man finished his dinner first, and he then told me to put the couple's entire dinner on his check. Today it would be well over $1,000 for that same meal. The instructions were not to let them know until he left the restaurant. My jaw dropped! It was like a Hollywood movie. When I told the couple, they were in shock!

Needless to say, I couldn't stop thinking about the scenario. Later in the evening, the person at the front desk said the man shared what a wonderful evening it had been and explained that he was married for over twenty years and had several children. He often traveled for business, and that night was the first time in his marriage that he had made a date with another woman. He was so relieved when she didn't show up! So, he wanted to do something special for the happy-looking couple at the next table. When he heard how they had long budgeted and planned for their 25th anniversary, that took it up another level. WOW! Who could have figured out that script? The anniversary couple got a fantastic surprise gift. And a husband had an opportunity to realize how much he loved his wife!

Here's the thing. If I had not seen life through the lens that the side-by-side unusual wine requests might not have been a coincidence, the discernment to offer a tasting might not have come. Also, what came up in me was, why bother? They might not be interested. But then the fun thought persisted, and I decided to check it out. Perhaps I was given a particular assignment to help others. If so, that is a great honor, privilege, and joy. Life is so much more than our own little world. There is a much bigger picture going on.

To Sommelier Or Not

One night, a young lady who had just turned twenty-one came to dinner with her parents at Del Frisco's. Her dad ordered a bottle of wine and suggested that she do the traditional sample tasting. When I gave her a sample pour to try, she got very emotional to the point of tears and said to me, "I feel so inadequate. What am I supposed to be tasting? How would you describe the wine?" The usual would have been for a sommelier to spout out words of wisdom describing the wine. However, I sensed a little encouragement to help her get over her fears would be so much better. Her parents were watching to see how I handled their daughter's vulnerability.

I said to her, "Let's try something. You taste the wine, say whatever comes to mind, and there are absolutely no right or wrong answers." Then I asked her if she noticed when tasting a fruit whether it was sweet and luscious or if it was tart? Or could she tell the difference between the texture of skim milk and whole milk? She replied, "Of course!"

I wasn't concerned about her being embarrassed. She tasted the wine, and I said her description was fantastic. I let her know it was better than what I would have offered. She knew I meant that and began to cry. Her parents were beaming from ear to ear. She was so proud of herself for both trusting to try and, to her surprise, discovering she had some hidden talent. As I enjoy doing, I threw in a little lighthearted humor. I asked if another customer asked me to describe that wine, did I have to give her credit, or could I just look brilliant giving them her description? We all laughed, and they let me know the evening was a great success. Little things can mean a lot. When I saw her vulnerability, I felt compassion, and a new idea emerged. It would have been so easy to just offer a description of the wine to calm the young lady's anxieties. Encouragement can be more rewarding than being a technical expert.

Soup's On

Then there was the time I was working as a server in a fine-dine restaurant with a celebrity chef. It was an intense environment, and I always felt like I was walking on eggs in dealing with the owners. The quality of the food was exceptional.

One day, a customer in a party of four asked my opinion about the soup of the day. That dish was an absolute standout specialty of the restaurant. I very enthusiastically encouraged the guest to try it. I came back to the table to see how he liked it. He had a big smile and said it was outstanding. Of course, I was excited and about to blurt out, "It sure beats Campbell's soup, doesn't it?"

That's my usual tableside humor. But before I could speak, I had a distinct thought—Don't say that! So, I kept quiet.

At the end of the meal, the guest introduced himself as CEO of Campbell's Soup. I almost fell over! I am quite confident that if he were offended and complained to the chef/owner, I would have been fired on the spot. Following that inner voice at the right time was "mmm, mmm good." Yes, that is the theme for Campbell's soup.

UNEXPECTED FRIENDSHIP

The timing of the 'so-called' coincidences in this story is unbelievable. It is about a long-time friend, Ed Lubin, a Jewish man whom I met 51 years ago in Los Angeles. He was originally from Pittsburgh, where his father owned a florist shop. Ed would sometimes make deliveries. On one occasion, at age 11, he was instructed to deliver flowers directly to the esteemed evangelist, Katherine Kuhlman, at her church. When he did, she took a moment to put a hand on his head and prayed for him.

Fast forward 25 years. Ed was working as sales manager for a radio station in Carmel, California. He needed a break and drove to Venice (Los Angeles) and stopped in a restaurant for breakfast. There (out of 24,000 restaurants in the metro area) he bumped into a former neighbor from Atlanta, Georgia, who invited him to a party that night. Mutual friends had also invited me to the same event where I met Ed for the first time. Strangely, Ed invited me to go back to Carmel with him for a visit. At first I declined. Then I heard it was so "peaceful" there and accepted. (It had been nine years with NO peace.) He and his girlfriend showed me care and kindness during my many physical illnesses and emotional struggles.

Six months later, Ed got fired, and he and his girlfriend found themselves in a cheap motel back in Los Angeles. He was very upset and threw his wallet against the wall. A tiny piece of paper with my phone number that I had given him months earlier fell on the floor. He immediately went to a pay phone to call me. A woman answered and said I had moved out a few months before. **At that exact moment,** there was a knock at her door. It was me coming to pick up something I had left there some time before! A minute or so either way, we would not have connected. I got on the phone, and Ed told me things weren't going well. I was glad to hear his voice.

By that time, my life had changed dramatically. Just the day before I was telling Doc about this guy Ed who had looked after me months earlier during my troubled times. Doc said there must have been a reason he was on your mind, so let's pray for him. How crazy is that! I drove to get Ed and his girlfriend so they could stay at my apartment. They were shocked to see the change in me.

Ed asked what had happened to me, but I didn't tell him. I took him to meet Doc. Ed immediately felt a strong connection, and when he asked, "What am I feeling?" Doc said, "It's Jesus." Ed said, "I'm Jewish, and that's not for me." The next day, Ed got turned down on a job interview he thought he was going to get. His situation hit him hard, and he felt like it was a low point in his life. Then as he was standing on the corner of Sunset Boulevard and Cahuenga in Hollywood, he heard a horn honking. It was a former mentor who offered Ed a job within the hour. The earnings were a salary and a 10% commission if Ed sold a TV show, which had not sold for a year. The asking price was $200,000. Ed set up a meeting in New York City to pitch the show.

The day before he left, he stopped by to visit Doc again who asked him why he was seemingly so upset and tense. Ed said he was trying to get back on his feet, and a few years earlier a "good friend" had cheated him out of $25,000. Doc asked, "What do you want?" Ed jokingly replied, "Well the $25,000 would be nice." Doc asked if Ed would mind if he prayed for him. He reached his hand toward Ed and said something like, "God, please give Ed $25,000 and let him know that you love him."

The group in New York wanted to buy the show and asked the price. For some reason, Ed blurted out $250,000 (more than what his boss wanted), and they agreed. When he reported back that he sold the show, he was told "You just made $25,000!" That's what it took for Ed to have an amazing life-changing experience that followed.

IT IS COMFORTING to know that you are not alone on the journey. Sometimes, when you are searching for an answer or are about to decide, you get a check. That means to hold on. You are on the wrong track. If you feel anxious and not peaceful, that could be a helpful indicator.

CHAPTER 9

THE JOURNEY CONTINUES

After finishing a consulting job a few years ago, I still needed to work. I saw a job posting for wine steward at one of the local Albertsons markets and contacted Tom Holloway, director for the store nearest me. He invited me to meet him, at which time he told me that job was filled. However, his eyes lit up when he heard both my passion for customer service and my wine background. He told me the company was in the process of building two new upscale destination stores (called Market Street) with exceptional wine programs, a restaurant, live music, and more. Although they were a few months away from posting any jobs, Tom called Brian Conley, store director of the first one to be finished. The interview went great, and, thanks to Brian, I was immediately hired. I even got to work from home, preparing for the opening a few months before the store was complete. Here's the point. I enjoy what I'm doing, and fun things keep happening. It seems to get even better, and I believe the best is yet to come.

MUSIC TO MY EARS

One day in the spring of 2019, I got an email from Tara at our corporate office asking to see if I could bring in Smokey Robinson Wines. I had no idea that Smokey had wines and got so excited because I've always been a huge fan of his and Motown. I immediately contacted Lou Caputo, one of Smokey's wine business team, who asked if Becky and I would like to come to a big food and wine festival at the Santa Monica Airport, where Smokey and Berry Gordy (founder of Motown) would be attending. Lou asked if I was familiar with the area. It was fun to tell him that Santa Monica was where Becky and I lived when we first got married. Also, as a private pilot, I used to fly out of that airport in a six-seat, single-engine Piper Saratoga that I co-owned with friends. The timing was especially interesting because I had told Becky just a few days prior that we needed to plan a trip soon to visit her then 92-year-old father, who lives in the LA area. So, I emphatically said yes! My wife and I had a fantastic time at the two-day event. We got to meet Smokey and other VIP members of the team, including Bob Buzzelli, business adviser; Matt Smith, award-winning winemaker; and Phil Quartararo, music industry executive. After the event, I arranged for Smokey's business team and winemaker to meet with the Albertsons wine management team at the corporate offices in Boise to discuss the possibility of bringing in their wines. To our surprise, Smokey came too. We were all so thrilled and agreed to launch four outstanding wines with beautiful silkscreen labels, each with the name of one of Smokey's songs: "Being With You" Pinot Noir, "Cruisin'" Red Blend, "I Second That Emotion" Cabernet, and "My Girl" Chardonnay. Smokey has written a tremendous number of songs for many artists. Bob Dylan called him "America's greatest living poet."

WE WERE ALL EXCITED, and the plan was for Smokey to come to Boise just before Christmas and do bottle signings and photo ops in both Market Street stores. Along the way, Lou and Bob invited Becky and me to be guests at Smokey's concert at the Wynn Resort in Las Vegas on September 21st, which just happened to be my birthday. What a fantastic and unexpected birthday present that turned out to be!

Smokey Robinson with my wife Becky and me at his Las Vegas
concert

Smokey did come to both stores that December. First, he met with the staff to sign bottles with personal messages and photo ops. Following that, the lines in the store to see him were incredible. He was so personable to every customer. To him, that meant asking everyone's name, what they wanted to be written on the bottle, hugs, and photos. We were concerned about how much time and energy it would take for him to see so many people in both stores. His attitude was that if they came to see him, he wanted to show his appreciation to everyone. It was a late night. What a guy!

It may be a radical concept to some that it's more than okay to enjoy life. I've learned to expect the unexpected in my journey, so I keep my eyes and ears open.

Trip Of A Lifetime

The trip of our lives came as a complete surprise. In the spring of 2019, Becky and I began discussing where to go on a vacation. Something I had always wanted to do was to take my wife to Europe, but it had never materialized. I mentioned the idea of going to Italy, but Becky didn't think she wanted to fly such a long distance. Then when we got an unsolicited invitation to visit the magnificent IL Borro medieval village in Tuscany for a few days, suddenly the flying concern went up in the air (pun intended). Becky knew this idea of a trip to Italy was getting real and had a sense the timing was meaningful. Then came the most dramatic surprise of all—an opportunity to extend our trip and go to Israel. Although we had always wanted to go, it hadn't happened. Going to Israel on this same trip never crossed our minds.

Our trip in October 2019 was extraordinary. After a long initial flight delay, we finally landed in Rome late in the afternoon. After checking into our hotel, Becky excitedly grabbed my hand to get going into the city. When she threw three coins into Trevia Fountain, our love affair with Italy officially began. The next stop was beautiful Florence. In advance of the trip, I had arranged to meet Roberto Becocci. He is the Italian national director for Stella Rosa, a high-quality, popular brand of sweeter wines. He and his darling wife Barbara took us to dinner at a historic hilltop restaurant overlooking the magnificent city lights.

Our greatly anticipated next stop was IL Borro in Tuscany in the province of Arezzo. Salvatore Ferragamo was a fantastic host, and our wine tasting in the gated cellar was outstanding. The stunning restored medieval village was like walking through a postcard—the beauty, the details, the history, the vast scenery—so much to take in. And the 1,000-year-old chapel was such an extraordinary surprise.

Next, we visited Castello d'Albola in Tuscany, a hilltop castle and winery property from the 12th century with incredible views and vineyards. They had no other guests, so they gave us the full upstairs of a centuries-old stone farmhouse inside the castle grounds (all complimentary). Are you kidding? They also said they were preparing for a VIP dinner event, would have extra, and insisted on serving us the three-course meal with wine in our quarters.

Then came our trip to Alba, where Roberto took us to a few extraordinary wineries. We booked a tour to go truffle hunting with a doggie, the guide, and an interpreter. We had a ball watching the dog searching for truffles, which are a wonderful delicacy. And we were taken to dinner in the city where we enjoyed fine wine and a special pasta dish with shaved truffles. The underground restaurant with curved stone and brick walls was like being in a wine cellar.

Verona is so beautiful, with a river going right through the middle of the city. The coliseum opera house was the highlight in the piazza, where a wonderful couple, Alberto and Dee Pecora, hosted us for dinner. They own Enovation brands, which are award-winning wines in attractive designer bottles. We got to see the very popular 1300s building and muse, Casa di Giulietta (Juliet's House), made famous in Shakespeare's Romeo and Juliet. And, of course, Venice, with its water taxis and gondola rides, was even more thrilling than we had imagined.

The Israel experience struck deep in both Becky and me. Our longtime dear friend, Ziva Ben-Reuven, hosted us at her high-rise condo in Tel Aviv, overlooking the city and the Mediterranean Sea. She lived and worked in the States for many years and had moved back to her home country. Ziva arranged several tours for us. It is hard to put into words what it meant to Becky and me to actually be in places we had read and heard so much about for years.

The Dead Sea is the lowest place on earth, about 1400 feet below sea level. The name comes from extreme saltiness, and it was fun to float with no effort. The hillside fortress of Masada was close by, and a cable car took us up to the historic site. What amazing views. But it was also a very sobering experience knowing the outcome of the chilling siege that once took place.

Being at the Sea of Galilee and Capernaum, where many miracles were recorded, was exciting! And this Jewish boy found a pastor to baptize him in the Jordan River.

Jerusalem, Jerusalem. Wow! In the Old City, we were fascinated by the closeness of the four quarters. Being at the Wailing Wall was so moving. It is well documented that this will be the place where the most significant events in world history will take place in the future!

As an added touch, we were privileged to be Ziva's guests at a concert by the world-class Israel Philharmonic. It turned out to be one of the last two performances by legendary conductor Zubin Mehta.

A month after returning home, Salvatore Ferragamo came to our Boise Albertsons stores to do wine tastings, bottle signings, and photo ops. He was very gracious, and many people enjoyed meeting him and learning about his wines. It was a blast.

With Salvatore Ferragamo presenting his IL Borro
wines in Boise

The trip to Italy and Israel was the adventure of our lives. It came about because Becky and I got an unexpected, unsolicited invitation and then the opportunity to go to Israel.

And how about timing? The worst flood in Venice since 1966 was the following month. Then, the COVID pandemic started just a few months later.

AND STILL IT CONTINUES

We thought our trip to Italy and Israel was the trip of a lifetime, and it was. Then came a bonus during the final stages of this book. It was another unsolicited, generous invitation by Pradorey

Winery, which became part of an amazing trip to Spain just after my 79th birthday.

We landed in Madrid, where a driver was waiting to take us to the magnificent Pradorey estate in Ribera del Duero during harvest. This historic property, originally a farm purchased by Queen Isabella in 1503, includes a former King's Palace where we stayed. There were a handful of other invited guests, and we had a great time, including picking grapes and crushing them barefoot. Juan Maestro Cuesta was the perfect host, and third-generation owner, Fernando Rodriguez Cremades de Rivera, gave us an exclusive winery tour and tasting.

Burgos is a beautiful and historic city. In the 1500s, it was the capital of Spain for a short time. Burgos Cathedral, built between 1221 and 1567, is the first Gothic cathedral in Spain. It is an architectural wonder filled with great art, wealth, treasures, and history. El Cid is buried there. It is the only independent cathedral in Spain to receive the UNESCO World Heritage Site designation. Just amazing and hard to describe in words.

Haro, a charming hilltop town, is the capital of Rioja, probably the most internationally known wine region in Spain. In advance of the trip, we had arranged VIP tours and tastings with three of the finest wineries in the country.

We had a group tour at beautiful La Rioja Alta Winery, followed by a private tour at Muga, hosted by David de la Fuente. We enjoyed being introduced to members of the founding family. Lunch on the patio included the most luscious tomatoes picked from their garden that morning, topped with their own olive oil and salt saturated with reserve red wine. Add to that, three clusters of ripe grapes that were in the white wine blend were served to enjoy with the meal—that was a first.

Christophe Chapillon then drove us on a gorgeous scenic route to Pedro Martinez Alesanco Winery. Set among the rolling hills of this gorgeous vineyard-laden countryside, we enjoyed fine wines and gracious family hospitality. The son, Pedro, who is running the winery, was our host. He introduced us to his mom (founding family), and his sister, who is the winemaker. Delightful!

San Sebastian is located on the Bay of Biscay in the heart of Basque region. It has magnificent beaches, natural beauty, and is abounding with a variety of architectural styles. This city also has more Michelin-Star restaurants per capita than any city in the world. For a special treat, I couldn't resist the opportunity to take Becky to one of them. Mirador de Ulia has a breathtaking hillside location overlooking the entire city and the sea. The food and service, which included a Master of Wine, were incredible. And the chef came out to meet us after our amazing meal. I must admit that after over twenty-five years in the food, wine, and hospitality industry, the experience brought a few tears to my eyes.

My wife has some French roots, so we decided to take a quick day trip to Biarritz, France, a 45-minute bus ride from San Sebastian. Biarritz is a beautiful, luxurious seaside resort in the Basque region of Southwest France. It is also enjoyed by worldwide surfers, and a competition was in progress that day. The five-star Hotel du Palais, built by Emperor Napoleon III for his wife, Empress Eugenie, has a long history of VIP guests, including Queen Victoria. We took a local bus tour to see the historic sites and enjoyed a little lunch overlooking the Bay. Magnifique!

A Mediterranean seaport, Barcelona is an amazing cultural, cosmopolitan, historic city, filled with an exciting lifestyle of shopping, great restaurants, and so many places to see. You can find Renaissance, Baroque, Gothic, and Art Nouveau architectural styles. It is the only city to ever receive the coveted RIBA Royal Gold Medal (1999) by the Institute of British Architects, which has been given only to individuals and groups since 1848. Perhaps the most famous architect was Antoni Gaudi. His central modern masterpiece is a cathedral, La Sagrada Familia. Construction began in 1905 and is expected to be completed in 2026. It is hard to describe in words… stunning, awe-inspiring, and amazing are the best I can do. The daughter of one of the attendees at my Albertsons wine classes was living in Barcelona. She graciously met us and showed us around. We also visited the Palau de la Música (Palace of Music), one of the most beautiful and breathtaking concert halls in the world and home to almost every genre of music. Many of the greatest singers, conductors, orchestras, and choirs have graced its stage. To name a few: Igor Stravinsky, Ella Fitzgerald, Zubin Mehta, Leonard Bernstein, Miles Davis, and the Sistine Chapel Choir. Many said playing the venue was "magical." And, of course, we could not visit Barcelona without seeing a Flamenco performance!

I still enjoy working and am fortunate to be the sommelier at Albertsons/Market Street in Boise, Idaho. And look what Becky and I would have missed if I hadn't decided to keep working at a later age. This is why I chose to share these exciting happenings. Life should be one continuous adventure, expansion, and love story.

Life In Long Island - Neighbor's Bar Mitzvah

My dad and mom (on right)

With Sammy Davis Jr. – I'm the tall guy in the back

Baseball great Mickey Mantle (left) and Nappy Grossbardt, co-founder of famous Colony Records on Broadway in New York City

World-renowned Killer Joe Piro Dance Team Performing

Me standing behind Billy Daniels, who was co-starring with
Sammy Davis Jr. in Golden Boy on Broadway

Our Families

My parents, Edie and Morty Walker, day of my bar mitzvah

In Denver with my brother Michael at 30-year celebration of church he started (December 3, 2021)

My dad, mom, me, sister Carol, brother Michael in Los Angeles (1970s)

Our Parents – Morty and Edie Walker, Pat and Bob Vernon

Becky's parents, Pat and Bob Vernon, on their film set at Universal Studios Hollywood (1950s)

Becky's mom Pat, Becky, dad Bob, sister Debbie, and brother Gregg (1970s)

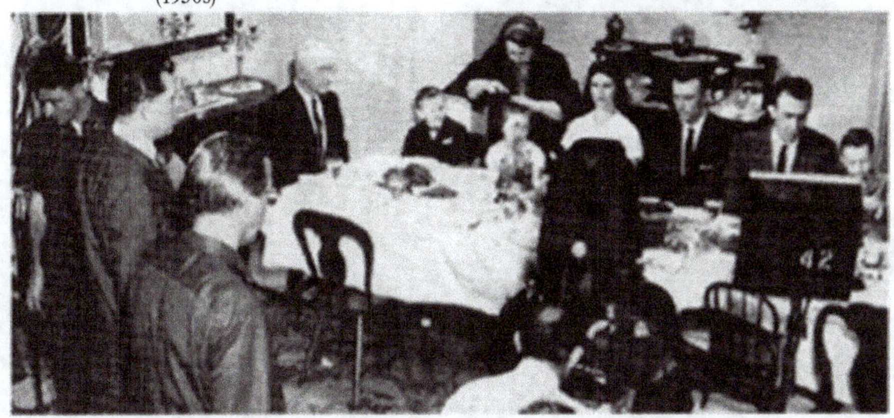

Vernon Family on Universal Studios set for their Homestead USA TV series—The cute little girl getting her hair styled before the scene is now my adorable wife.

Becky and her dad (right) on Vietnam USO tour (1967)

Stephen and Becky, Wedding Day (1985)

Our daughter Jessica and her husband Darrin, Wedding Day (2017)

Our son Jeremy and his wife Lashai, Wedding Day (2020)

Vow Renewal - 35th Anniversary

The Happy Couple

My "proposal"—finally!

Oh how we danced.

Celebration toast by Salvatore and Tini Ferragamo via Zoom from IL Borro Chapel in Tuscany, Italy

Trips of a Lifetime
~Italy~

Stephen at the Roman Colosseum

Becky in beautiful Verona

Overlooking Florence

Stayed at Castello di Albola, a 15th century castle, now an inn and winery in Chianti, Tuscany

~Italy~

With Salvatore Ferragamo at IL Borro, his family's 1700-acre restored
medieval village, 5-star resort, and award-winning winery, Tuscany

IL Borro, Tuscany

A gondola ride in Venice

Truffle hunting in Alba

~Israel~

With dear friend, Ziva Ben-Reuven, on her balcony in Tel Aviv overlooking the city and Mediterranean Sea

Our first look at Jerusalem

Synagogue at Capernaum where many
miracles once took place

Me being baptized in the Jordan River

~Israel~

Stephen and Becky at Wailing Wall, Jerusalem

At Sea of Galilee

Masada National Park – scene of a
dramatic, historic battle

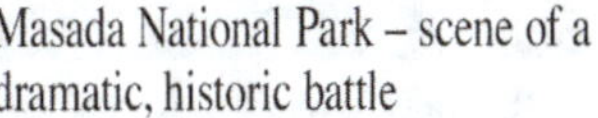

Floating in The Dead Sea

~Spain~

Mirador de Ulia Michelin-Star restaurant view,
San Sebastian

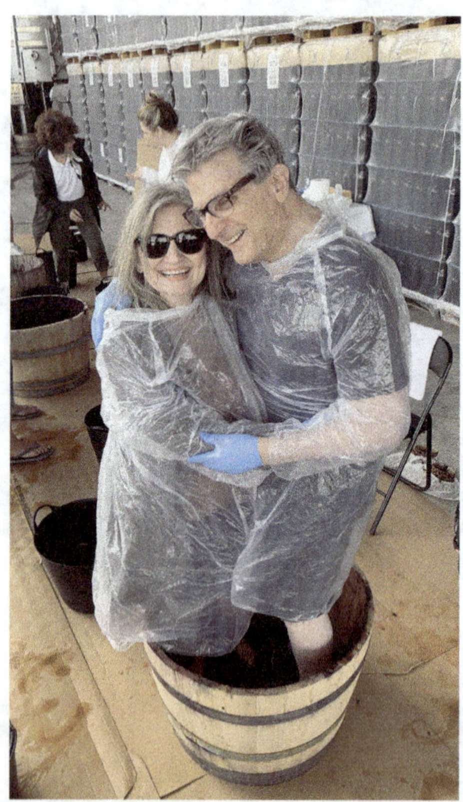

Crushing grapes, Pradorey Winery harvest

Hilltop view of Burgos and famous Cathedral

City Square of Haro, wine capital of Rioja

Sagrada Familia
Cathedral, Barcelona

Hotel Los Augustinos in Haro,
built as a convent in 1373,
became a military hospital in
1811, now a fine hotel

Becky at Palau de Musica (Palace of Music), Barcelona

PART THREE

HOW DOES IT WORK
IN RELATIONSHIPS?

CHAPTER 10

CROSSING CULTURAL BARRIERS

BOLD AUTHORITY

I was invited to go to Africa in 1964, and it was a nightmare. Many years later, I got an unsolicited, unexpected invitation to return. It was the most exciting trip of my life! At my sommelier job, people came into the restaurant from countries I had visited, which led to amazing relationships. I believe these things could not have happened unless they were orchestrated.

In 1981, I was working as a server in Los Angeles, but was between jobs with no savings in the bank. My dad called and said he thought it was time for me to take over his successful lithography business in Manhattan. I thanked him for the kind offer, then told him my life was so fulfilling and exciting that I didn't want to leave.

A few weeks later, I got a job as a server in an African restaurant. Before starting, I was challenged to drop everything and make an immediate plane reservation to Accra, Ghana. The teaser was that my good friend, Johnny Baker, was heading to Ghana with another group, and I could meet up with him.

Everyone who knew my 1964 trip to Africa had been filled with death and despair was so happy for me to go. They lent me the money, and it all did get paid back. Two others decided they also wanted to go. It was Saturday, so we had to race to the airport to get the required overseas vaccinations.

At that time, there were significant airline strikes worldwide. We managed to book a flight to New York for the following morning. But at the airport, one flight after the other was canceled. So, what did we do? Of course, we prayed. It took a while, but at last, we boarded the plane. That was just the beginning of our adventure.

We stayed with our friend in New York City. Going from one airline ticket agency to another, we had to wait in long lines only to find out no flights to Ghana were available. Even sharing the exciting adventure we were on didn't help, until we got to TWA. The agent seemed moved by our story; however, she apologized that she couldn't help. Suddenly, her jaw dropped. She said, "I've never seen anything like this, but three seats [to Ghana via London] just came open!" We all, including the agent, jumped up and down, cheering.

Then, the flight to London was so delayed that we missed our connecting flight to Ghana. In order to use our tickets for another flight, we had to get one of the airlines to certify them. Refused by about twenty airlines, I didn't give up. Finally, we got an authorized change to go to Lagos, Nigeria, and on to Ghana. Upon arrival in Lagos… you guessed it. We missed our connecting flight to Ghana and were told the next available flight would be in two or three days. We thought there had to be something better, so we approached many other airlines for help. Air India said they could get us on a flight only if we allowed them to list us as cargo instead of passengers. Am I kidding? No. Hooray, we finally made it to Accra! A few days later, two friends who had just gotten married decided to come and somehow found us. We located Johnny Baker by chance. Was it ever good to finally be together!

One night, a group of us drove to a community in Tema and had an impromptu meeting. That meant a few of the Ghanaian team started playing music, and shortly a crowd gathered. We all shared, and everyone had a great time. On the way back, we passed a checkpoint where two policemen with rifles approached our car. One of them stuck his head in the window to ask where we had come from and where we were going. We openly told him. He then tauntingly said, "Why don't you pray for us to get powerful, rich, and famous?" One of the girls said, "He's drunk. Can you smell his breath?"

Instantly, without thinking, I jumped out of the car and walked over to them as they tightly held their rifles. I said something like: *You guys are making a mockery. We're talking about the Kingdom of Heaven. It's so much bigger than fame and money. Just before I came here, I turned down becoming a millionaire to come to Africa with almost no money. This is so much bigger!* They looked stunned, and when I didn't get shot, I headed to the car. They asked me to stop and come back. I thought this could be real trouble but turned around. They both dropped their rifles and told me their lives were a mess. They bowed their heads and asked me to pray for them. I was not expecting that at all! Meanwhile, my friends in the car couldn't believe what they were watching, including the other cars going by the checkpoint without being stopped.

A few weeks earlier, I had turned down my dad's substantial financial offer with no clue that I'd be in Africa sharing that story with two policemen holding rifles—really? People in a position of authority understand a higher authority. What came from within me had power and truth, which were respected. I had made a heart choice (essential component) to put something bigger above money, giving me authority. My concern was for them. When I got out of the car, I had no fear, anger, or judgment. I would not have gotten out had I felt any of those. Rather, it was more like *snap out of it and get real.*

FINDING AN OASIS

A businessman, Jori Adu, heard about our group and invited all six of us to be guests in his home with his family. One day he asked me to please go to the American Embassy to appeal for some water. He explained that the entire region was experiencing a dire water emergency. I asked him why he chose me. He answered that he thought I could do it. Although it was hard for me to comprehend being without water (it did not compute), I agreed to go.

When I arrived and introduced myself, the head of the embassy told me off and said in effect: *Are you crazy? There's a severe water shortage, you just got here, and you want water— NO WAY!* My typical response would be to make a strong appeal; however, I stood completely silent (be assured, not the usual). My focus was on the reality that our host family needed water, and I was not leaving until that happened. Within seconds, the Ambassador started yelling, "Get him a truck, get him 1,500 gallons of water, get him out of here!" It was dramatic and unexpected but so exciting to get back to the cheers of friends and the family!

It was an eye-opening revelation to understand how a discernment (for me to be silent) can work without words. First came the thought of compassion for our host family. Then came a clear impression to be still. I'm a talker, but that's not always how it works. I recognized that it wasn't my usual response, and I became silent. As soon as I got out of the way, it happened.

Opening Prison Doors

Two of the Ghanaian team were former prisoners on death row in Nsawam Prison. Each of them had miraculous, life-changing experiences while in prison, and they were released. In order for our group to have meetings there, we needed to get permission. I'm not sure why I was chosen to go. It was a little surreal going to the head of prisons in a foreign country and asking to get into the prison. It turned out to be an adventure beyond my expectations.

I got dropped off by car at an old building that required climbing a wooden staircase. I sensed a bizarre, foreign weight on my being. It was physically hard to move. We had been informed that at times in Africa we would have these very strange feelings. I recognized where it was coming from. It's called witchcraft. Unless you've been there, it may be hard to comprehend.

With both hands on the rails, I had to pull myself up the staircase. The weight I felt was that heavy. I had no appointment and approached the receptionist. She told me the prison director was away for the day and would not be back until the following morning. It hadn't been easy to get a ride and no way did I want to come back. I asked if I could just sit and wait. The receptionist repeated that he was not expected to return until the following morning but politely said I may sit.

The intense weight persisted, and all I knew to do was pray silently. After about fifteen minutes, I felt a release, like someone who had been standing on my chest just got up. It was a dramatic change in an instant. Right after that, the receptionist called to me, "Mr. Walker, to our complete surprise, the director has returned, and he will see you." I can only share that I knew I had been given the authority to accomplish my mission.

His name was Director Gerald Acquaah-Gaisie. He had more medals on his uniform than I had seen in any movie. It was a display of power that could easily intimidate anyone. He asked the purpose of my visit and how he could help. I felt this bold authority that even surprised me. I cut right to it and told him that we were a small group of friends from the States working with a few local Ghanaians and that we needed his permission to go into Nsawam (medium security) prison.

Without hesitating or asking any questions, he said okay and then asked if there was anything else? I said, "Yes. You need to give us an official document with our names on it, sign it, and put your seal on it."

He said, "I will do that. Is there anything else?"

"Yes," I replied. "You need to do the exact same thing for the girls who are with us so they can go into the women's prison." He then opened the door and called in his assistant deputy director. He told his associate to take me with him and do whatever I said. They then created the documents, signed them, and added their official seal. The session with the director took about three minutes. It was wild. These official documents allowed us to have several meetings in the prisons, and they were remarkable.

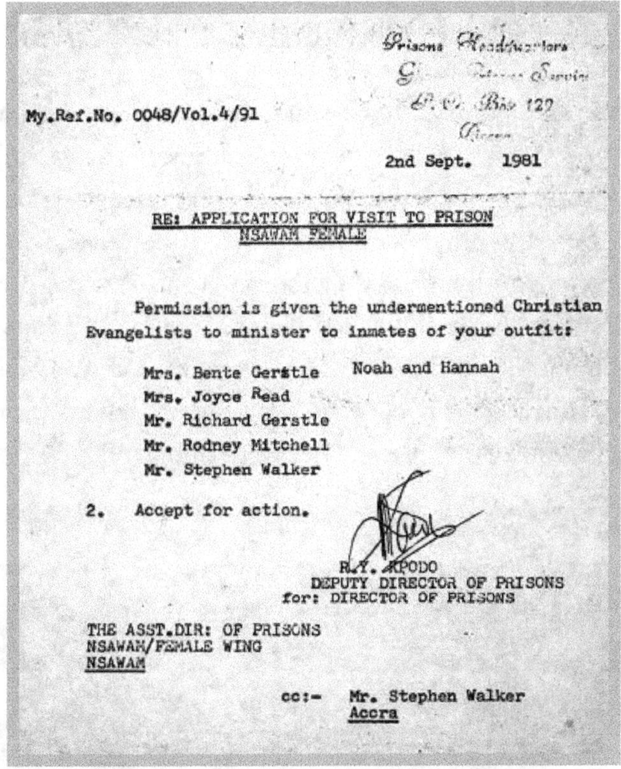

My.Ref.No. 0048/Vol.4/91

2nd Sept.   1981

RE: APPLICATION FOR VISIT TO PRISON
NSAWAM FEMALE

Permission is given the undermentioned Christian
Evangelists to minister to inmates of your outfit:

Mrs. Bente Gerstle   Noah and Hannah
Mrs. Joyce Read
Mr. Richard Gerstle
Mr. Rodney Mitchell
Mr. Stephen Walker

2.   Accept for action.

R.Y. APODO
DEPUTY DIRECTOR OF PRISONS
for: DIRECTOR OF PRISONS

THE ASST.DIR: OF PRISONS
NSAWAM/FEMALE WING
NSAWAM

cc:-   Mr. Stephen Walker
Accra

Miraculously, the prison official gave written
permission for our group to minister in the prisons!

A Glorious Cloud

In the final stage of this book, my very dear friend Johnny Baker passed away, making this story all the more meaningful to me. He and I had an exceptionally close, deep, caring friendship for more than 45 years. During one of the prison meetings, Johnny and I had the opportunity to share together in front of a room full of prisoners and guards. I shared my story first, and it was well received.

When Johnny spoke, he opened his heart, and with tears rolling down his cheeks, he shared his profound gratitude and love for how his life dramatically changed after meeting my friends. It was very powerful, and all of a sudden, there was such an exhilarating presence in the room, that the prisoners jumped out of their seats and started singing and dancing with incredible joy! The prison guards came over to us and said in so many words that they wanted to have the same experience because the prisoners were freer than they were!

One of our group, Dicky Gerstle, who was sitting off to the side, came over to me and asked if I saw the cloud come into the room. Although I did not see it, he assured me it was visible and palpable. That confirmed what we already knew. Something beyond happened. Johnny and Dicky are in this picture.

Wonderful trip to Ghana, West Africa (1981) with great friends: Rod Mitchell (4th row center, tall guy), Johnny Baker (to Rod's left), Dicky Gerstle (2nd row, 5th from left), me (2nd row, 3rd from right, striped tie)

Déjà Vu

We had another meeting scheduled at James Fort prison in the afternoon. But, by the end of the first meeting, one of the girls with us who was pregnant was experiencing morning sickness.

We were in a bind. How could we possibly get her back to the house and get to the other meeting? Suddenly, Mr. Nkansah, who had introduced us to the two former prisoners, showed up. I rushed over to meet him and shared our dilemma. He smiled and, in a very soft, humble tone, said, "I know. This morning in a vision, I saw that she was sick. That's why I changed my plans and came. I will take her home."

The group of us piled into our car and headed to the next meeting. And wouldn't you know, the car broke down. We anxiously tried to hitchhike, but nobody would stop. Most of the passing cars were full. We were on top of a slight incline. I took one of the Ghanaian team with me and went down the hill. A few minutes later, a man in a pickup truck stopped. We told him our situation, and he said he would be happy to take us to our destination. I jumped in the front seat and explained that more people were waiting on top of the hill. He said it was no problem, and he would take all of us. I couldn't resist asking why he stopped.

He told us he was the pastor of a church, and that morning he felt too sick to conduct the service. He so wished he could still help others that day and fell back asleep. He said he had a dream and clearly saw a broken-down car and our faces. As soon as he saw us, he knew that we were the ones in his dream. In addition, he had been trying to get into James Fort prison for a few years to have meetings but had been unable to make the connection. After that day, it was possible. He was so excited, and we were overjoyed.

COMMUNICATING BEYOND WORDS

One night, Mr. Adu arranged for six of us to go to a remote village where he had built a church. It was a thatched hut. We wholeheartedly agreed to go. He told us they knew we were coming. I said, "Great. You've already called them." He answered, "No, they don't have phones. They will sense that we are coming with goodwill, and their hearts will be open when we arrive."

By that time, I just trusted that what he said was so. It was a wild drive over bumpy roads. When we arrived, a group of people met us as if we were lifelong dear friends, just like Mr. Adu said. We had an interpreter when we spoke. The best part was when we sang, danced, and hugged. So much love and joy abounded. At the end of the evening, they gave us a beautiful basket of fruit.

When we got back to Mr. Adu's house, he sat us all down. He pointed to the basket of fruit and said, "Do you see that?" Of course, we saw it. He said, "They gave you their food for the week." Our jaws dropped. We immediately protested that we couldn't take it. He said, "That's why I waited until we got home to tell you. If you had refused their gift, it would have hurt them." Talk about us getting a lesson in love and gratitude.

He also said that while we were singing and dancing in the hut, a full-fledged witchcraft meeting was happening in another part of the village. We were glad not to know about it at the time. Mr. Adu said one of the men from the witchcraft meeting came and stood next to him, looking through the window. He turned to Mr. Adu and said, "I have never seen anything like that in my life. That's what my life will be about from now on."

Africa has a long history of witchcraft practices. When people there turn to a life of caring for others, that spiritual area inside them is more fertile. Discernment is a little more natural. It was explained that another reason they can sense so many things is because it is a matter of life and death. With ongoing tribal warfare, they have to know when danger is on the way. You can't make this stuff up.

OH, THAT LAUGHTER!

Almost everyone has heard the expression that the truth will set you free. It can release joy as well. One day during the trip, I walked to a rural market. Along the way, a group of kids around eight to ten years old were laughing and pointing at me, saying, "Oblani, oblani." When I got home and told our host, Mr. Adu, he explained that they were saying white man, white man. He assured me they were so happy and excited because they almost never saw white people. He also told me if I saw them again to point my finger and say obibini, which means little black man.

I couldn't wait to go again, and there they were in the same place. As soon as I pointed and said, "Obibini, obibini," they all went into hysterics. Some of them fell to the ground holding their sides and laughing. It was refreshing and wonderful to see what differences are really like without prejudice… joy! I wish I had a video of them. On a personal note, anyone who has been to Africa would likely agree that the kids are so adorable. They melt your heart and are so much fun to be around. What an exciting, encouraging, and revealing eye-opener.

IT'S ABOUT TIME

During that trip, we saw discernment in action in a practical way. A few friends who had been there the prior year learned that two men they liked a lot had a falling out and hadn't spoken to each other in a year. They managed to reach each of them individually and arranged a meeting at our house one night at 6:00 p.m. The hope was to get them together so they could reconcile. They both agreed, but neither one of them showed up. The funny thing is both of them arrived at 6:00 p.m.—two days later! They assured us they had not spoken to one another but knew that was the right moment. Reconciliation was achieved, and everyone was happy. Welcome to *Africa time*! Who needs a watch or a clock? Wouldn't that be nice?

A DOCTOR'S TRUE GREATNESS

One day in 1982, the year after returning from Africa, I was surprised when Mr. Nkansah called from Ghana, especially since international phone systems at that time were sketchy. During our Ghana trip, we spent time with him and his two sons, who wound up attending university in the States. He was a fine man, very caring, and through him, we met some outstanding people. After the call, I left for work at L'Escoffier. It was a busy night, and we had two sommeliers on the floor. My associate asked me to take care of one of his tables. The host spoke with an accent, and I asked where he was from. When he said Ghana, I got so excited. I briefly told him about my trip and the phone call I received just before work. He said that was fantastic and we needed to get together.

His name was Dr. Peter Bright-Asare, and I later learned that he was one of the leading gastroenterologists and researchers in the world. His bio included so many achievements, honors, and awards that it was hard to imagine one person could do all that. Peter was a bigger-than-life person and always upbeat. He came from Ghana to Canada, Chicago, and then Los Angeles, where he was given the keys to the city by Mayor Tom Bradley. We became good friends and fed off each other's enthusiasm and zeal for life, including good music.

A few years after we met, I got word that Peter, in his late fifties, died suddenly. It was a terrible shock, and at his funeral, filled with so much love and great respect, I learned a few things that made me realize even more why it was such a privilege to know him. Dr. Bright-Asare had purchased a medical research system from me (Doc's heart pump) at a significant cost. One of his associates told me that although he really hadn't had any current use for the system, he bought it because he thought it would help me. They also told me that the investment was a financial sacrifice! I was stunned and greatly humbled.

I later discovered that about seven to eight years before his death, a bus had gone out of control on an icy Chicago freeway, and Peter's lungs were filled with diesel fuel, which caused significant respiratory problems from that time forward. Although he was told he would only live five to ten years after that, he never once mentioned it to me. When it got really bad, and he knew his life was coming to an end, he gathered his staff from Drew King Medical Center, and they performed medical procedures around the clock at no charge!

When people are at the end of life, what's truly important to them becomes the total focus. For Dr. Bright-Asare, it was wanting to give the best of his medical abilities to help others in need and who couldn't afford to pay. Regardless of your age, take a few minutes to think about what you would do if you were given a report that you had six months to live. You may be surprised.

Undercover Ambassador

One night, a man came into L'Escoffier, and when I approached his table, he began speaking to me in French. Since I know a little of that language, I thought it would be fun to ask him in French where he was from. When he told me Gabon, West Africa, I got very animated. You may recall that's where I was heading when I was given crash instructions. I hadn't met anyone from Gabon, and I was amazed to remember enough French to share my story. I knew he was following me because when I got stuck on the word to describe how the clouds parted, he filled in "miracle," the same word in French as in English. When I finished, he said in perfect English, "That is a great story!" Taken aback, I asked why he didn't tell me he spoke English. He said he was so enjoying me giving everything I had to speak French.

He then introduced himself as the Ambassador from Gabon, living in the Embassy in Washington, DC. There, sitting at my table, was the Ambassador to the small (population around two million) French-speaking country in Africa where I almost died. With hundreds of fine restaurants in the area, he chose this one. How did he know I spoke French? And how did I recall the words when I didn't practice speaking it?

He told me that his daughter, Francine, was attending university in Los Angeles and asked if I would kindly meet and look out for her. He said the only other person he trusted her with was a lady from Brazil. I was humbled and honored and greatly appreciated his ability to read me so quickly. Of course, I said yes. I also asked Johnny and Jo Ann to be involved, and we had some great times with Francine. Jo Ann became especially close with her, which meant a lot to Francine.

Yet the Gabon saga didn't end. A few months later, the Ghanaian friend who was instrumental in arranging our 1981 trip to Ghana came out from New York City to Los Angeles for a visit. He said he wanted me to help him meet with Madam Bongo, then First Lady of Gabon, who was staying in the area. I couldn't believe what I was hearing as he explained that he had an urgent, high-security message to deliver. When he said he wanted us to go to her house and knock on the gate, I told him it could be a considerable risk. That was over thirty years ago. These days, forget about it.

That seemed like a Hollywood script, and I wasn't sure about the ending. Charmer that he was, Daniel convinced me to go. Part of my saying yes was the recent meeting with the Ambassador. I announced ourselves at the gate, and, in French, I mentioned the Ambassador's name and said we had an important message for her. To our surprise, the gate opened, and we were invited in! She was a very gracious and charming hostess; however, I chose to go into another room while Daniel delivered the message. What you don't know won't hurt you. I didn't want to know. When I came back into the room, there was a personable get-together, which was a real treat. Daniel later told me the message was well received.

During that same time period, a severe and devastating drought was happening in Africa. Daniel formed the Africa Drought & Disaster Relief Organization to help raise support for food, clothing, and medical supplies to alleviate the crisis. Johnny Baker and I assisted in the effort, including a trip to Washington, DC, and me getting a booth at a convention.

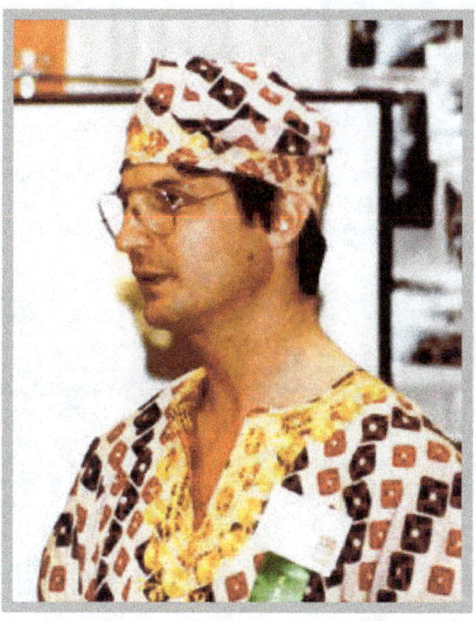

Wearing my Ghanaian outfit at a convention booth, I shared the need for relief during a severe drought in Africa.

CHAPTER 11

MARRIAGE—OURS AND YOURS

MEET THE PARENTS

My good-looking parents, Morty and Edie Walker, were from the Bronx, New York. Dad lost his mother at age twelve, and although he skipped several grades to graduate from high school at age fourteen, he chose to help support the family by going right to work. He eventually started his own color lithography business in New York City, which became very successful. His clients included Estee Lauder, Revlon, and the Museum of Modern Art. He was recognized as an industry leader for the highest standards of color work, as well as for pioneering the duotone black process. That technique allowed black-and-white photos to have a much deeper richness. My mom's father and mother emigrated from Kiev, Ukraine, and Moldova, respectively. Her parents lost three children to the plague in Europe, and her father turned to God for solace. He was very devout and built a Jewish synagogue in the Bronx. Mom had a deep, sensitive side to her and a terrific laugh. She would crack up laughing at her own jokes, which would send people into hysterics.

I am fortunate to have fantastic in-laws. We hit it off the minute we met. What an attractive couple, Bob and Pat Vernon, who grew up on small-town farms in middle America. I enjoyed my mother-in-law, beautiful on the inside and out. She was always welcoming, a fabulous cook, and her giggle was contagious. My father-in-law, a WWII Navy submarine veteran and one of seven brothers, became a minister along with three brothers. The four of them also sang together, and, amazingly, they each married a woman who sang their exact counterpart. They traveled worldwide and recorded several albums.

Bob pioneered the first Christian family television series, *Homestead USA*, filmed at Universal Studios. Featuring three generations of the Vernon family, episodes included scripted acting, singing, and Bible teaching. The series was so successful that the entire family was invited to appear on an episode of the popular weekly live show, *I've Got a Secret* hosted by Gary Moore. Johnny Carson happened to be a guest panelist that night. Their appearance received the highest positive response of any episode up to that time.

Something extraordinary happened to my parents in their 70s. Although they and Becky's parents were from totally different worlds, we were amazed at how much they loved and cared for each other like brothers and sisters. Over time, my parents so trusted my father-in-law, Bob, that he was able to share his faith with them.

In 1996, our family lived in Glendale, Arizona, and both sets of parents came to visit. While Becky and I were out, Bob was sharing thoughts from the Bible and asked my mom if she wanted to be baptized. She replied no because she felt it would be a betrayal to her father. Then Bob carefully explained how it would actually be a fulfillment of what is written in the Old Testament.

Something broke in my mother, and she said, "Let's do it." Then my father said he didn't want to be left out. When Becky and I got home and heard what was happening, I almost fell over, partly because of something that had happened many years earlier when my father got so upset during a conversation about God that he suffered a stroke. Fortunately, he recovered, but it was a long, hard road for him after that. And things weren't easy for my mom.

Now here we were at this moment. We all went out to our pool. Bob baptized both of my parents, as well as our two children who had always wanted their "Poppa" to be the one to baptize them. To me, it seemed surreal but was a celebration for everyone. The next morning at breakfast, I asked my dad if he wanted to say a prayer. Mind you, I had never heard my dad pray in my whole life. He opened his heart like a child, with such purity and innocence. Tears rolled down his cheeks as he expressed profound gratitude for what had happened to him. We all lost it. There is always hope. It truly does spring eternal.

Our Marriage

How did I go from being a confirmed bachelor to a happy marriage? It took a lot of help along the way just to get to the altar. In gratitude, I want to share our story with the hope of bringing you much love and joy.

In August 1974, Becky and I met in the library of an Italian-style villa in Pacific Palisades, California. Becky says that when she saw me, she felt an attraction but thought I might be trouble. I had no clue. At that time, Becky was just coming out of a broken marriage with an unfaithful husband. We became good friends.

A couple of years later, we were in that same library with a room full of friends socializing and looking at photos on a screen. Becky was sitting directly opposite me on the other side of the room. When I looked up and saw her, I suddenly felt this overwhelming, incredible love, unlike anything I'd ever experienced! It was so sweet, unexpected, and powerful that it shook me up. I was desperately trying to cope and wondered what in the world was happening. I was sitting on an oversized chair, and for some crazy reason, this thought came to me: *If she gets up and asks to sit down next to me, my life will never be the same.* She then got up and began walking across the room. I was shaking inside. She said that it was hard to see the screen from where she was and asked if she could share the seat with me. I had to do everything I could to gather myself.

Soon after, I asked her out on a date. And we dated, and dated, and dated. After several years, some friends sat me down to say that I was stuck and needed to propose. That made logical sense. So, I proposed in the High Sierras under a full moon. She said yes. The next morning, I woke up terrified and told Becky that being engaged just wasn't real to me. That was a terrible thing on my part and caused Becky a lot of hurt. Although we remained in the same group of friends, we hardly spoke for some time.

On Valentine's Day in 1985, our friend who was getting ready to go on his honeymoon challenged me to get Becky some flowers. My first reaction was how could he dare suggest that, knowing we weren't even together at the time. I almost immediately realized I was still in love with her. I raced to the store and dropped off flowers where she worked. When I didn't hear from her, I called the front desk, and they told me she had gone home early. So, I quickly picked up the flowers and dropped them off at her home. The next day she called to say thank you. She was hesitant, but the fire soon rekindled, and we started dating—again.

A few months later, Becky said, "Stephen, if you don't know by now, go jump in a lake!" I knew this time she really meant it. That night at my L'Escoffier sommelier job, I was a basket case. I went to the empty back room of the restaurant, kicked a trash can, and looked up, saying, "Please help me get over my pride in proposing."

Becky gave me this sign as a reminder of her
ultimatum when I hadn't proposed after nine years!

Unbeknownst to me, Becky was with friends entertaining an overseas guest in the library where it had all begun when she was asked if I had proposed yet. She said no and didn't expect what followed. It was teasingly suggested that to put herself out of lingering misery, why not just call me at work and get a final answer so she could get on with her life. Then some of the girls excitedly brought her the phone.

Back at the restaurant, someone yelled, "Stephen, are you there? Becky's on the phone for you." She never called me at work, and I shouted to ask her to hold. I tried to gather myself. As soon as I got on the phone, she said, "I have a question for you."

I replied, "What is it?" (Remember, earlier that day, she told me to go jump in a lake!)

Then she said, "Will you marry me?"

I blurted out, "I'd love to. When?" (What a crazy way to say yes!)

I heard a big roar of laughter and cheers in the background.

Boy, I didn't expect that answer, especially so fast. For the rest of the evening, I ran around the restaurant telling all the customers I had just gotten engaged over the phone and that SHE was the one who proposed. They kept pouring wine into my tasting cup to join in a toast of celebration!

We set the date for August 18th. Along the way, we were given sound advice not to start a marriage by going into debt. You may recall the Beverly Hills judge giving us the same advice. So, we planned to have a simple ceremony at Becky's parent's condo in Sherman Oaks. I was also given specific advice to redeem my bride. At the time, I didn't understand what that meant. Over the years, the meaning has unfolded. WOW!

The day before our wedding, a gathering was held for us at the Villa. Becky directed a choir, and they chose a special song for my mother. When it was then lightheartedly suggested that I go to the top of the spiral staircase and sing a love song to my bride, I thought it was a joke because I couldn't carry a tune. Just about every time I tried to sing, I was told to stop because it was off-key. But I was so full of love for my bride-to-be that I took the challenge. Somehow, I managed to open my heart and sing with love from my spirit. It was a first and a beyond experience for me! Becky said all the girls were so touched that they were crying. Maybe she also thought if this guy could do that in front of all our friends, everything would go well. That same day, Becky and I received some advice that sounded so simple yet proved invaluable: ***If you focus on The Love and not each other, all will go well.***

The next day, Judge Burns, dressed in his black judge's robe, along with his lovely wife Mildred, joined us to deliver their wedding gift—performing a wonderful and personalized ceremony.

Early in our marriage, Becky and I were having a disagreement in a normal tone of voice. All of a sudden, she smacked me. It was completely unexpected for both of us, to say the least, and it was the first time we had experienced that in our individual lives. Then, amazingly, I instantly felt complete peace and was concerned for her. We both realized that something in our conversation had triggered a deep hurt from her first marriage, and she trusted me enough for her to let it fly. She was utterly shocked and embarrassed, but the situation provided an opportunity for me to give her reassuring love. We laugh about it to this day.

Becky, at age thirty-five, was so excited to have our first baby. It would have been a home birth, except we lived too far from the birth center. One evening a few days past the due date, Becky called me at work having more frequent contractions. I got home very quickly. Before we left for the birth center, Becky flipped from doing fine to feeling some fear and tension. She grabbed me and said, "What do I do?" I felt lost. Then a thought came. I said one word, "Trust." It was fascinating to watch her immediately transform from fear to calm within minutes.

When we got to the birth center on September 4, 1986, the team said she looked so good that she couldn't possibly be ready to give birth. She did look beautiful. After a quick exam, they decided she was ready. I thought, why not bring in a little humor? Easy for me. I wasn't the one giving birth. Between contractions, I said something silly to make Becky laugh. Then how she beamed when holding our son, Jeremy David. I couldn't believe I was a dad. The birthing team said that was one of their best experiences.

On October 24, 1988, just before Becky's 38th birthday, our second child, Jessica Ruth, was born at home with the same nurse and midwife. Now my wife has a sense of humor and is very practical. She awakened me very early in the morning having some contractions and wanted me to time them while she trimmed my hair, saying I needed to look good for the pictures. Are you kidding? So, I complied, of course. Anything for my wife about to give birth. I was ecstatic just a few hours later to announce, "It's a girl!" Becky was once again amazing.

In the early 1990s, I sold animated Bible and historic family educational video programs with workbooks for the kids. We would set up kiosks in malls, play the videos on a TV, and explain the program to passing customers. I sold between three and six sets almost every day.

One time, Becky and I were having a disagreement about her having to work full time. She really felt the need to be home with our young kids. I kept stubbornly refusing her request. After three days of no sales, I knew something was wrong. I walked to a private area and called Becky to apologize and surrender. When I got back to the kiosk, a family was waiting to buy a set. Sales didn't happen that way, and I was thrilled to get a very clear message. The moment I decided to be loving, I made a sale without having to say a word. This verse from the Bible came to life for me: "Husbands… be considerate as you live with your wives and treat them with respect… and as heirs with you of the gracious gift of life, so that nothing will hinder your prayers" (I Peter 3:7). I will be sharing other verses that are also filled with inspiration and, of most importance, life-changing power!

My mom and dad, a few family members, and close friends were together following Becky's parents' 50th wedding anniversary. I got up to give a toast, going on and on expressing my gratitude for all kinds of things, when my dad shouted, "And thank God for Becky!" Oh boy, that obviously should have been first on my list. The room went into hysterics. I was so embarrassed.

~

WHILE WE WERE LIVING in Franklin, Tennessee, there was a particular point that I thought I really needed to get across to Becky. I just couldn't understand why she wasn't able to see it. The stalemate went on for several days. I finally said that we needed to sit down and get through it and thought I had made my case. She responded with one sentence. Instantly I got it. I was the one who was blind. Very shaken, I went into another room and sobbed profusely, face down on the carpet, for over an hour. I realized that I had been judging her about something and couldn't even see it. After that, I felt much more care and appreciation for her. I am so grateful that my wife never gives up. It has helped me trade pride for love and joy on more occasions than I can count.

OVER THE YEARS, we talked about the possibility of doing a vow renewal ceremony. Becky had always wanted to have one in a church or chapel since our simple wedding was at her parents' condo. In October 2019, we were guests of Salvatore Ferragamo at IL Borro, his family's medieval village and winery estate in Tuscany, Italy. It includes a magnificent historic chapel, which especially impressed Becky with its atmosphere and details. The next month, Salvatore came to Boise to promote his IL Borro wines with me at the Albertsons Market Street stores. He invited Becky and me to dinner that night. I mentioned that the following year would be our 35th anniversary, and I hoped we could do a vow renewal ceremony. Salvatore suggested that perhaps we could return to IL Borro and have the ceremony in their chapel. What a kind suggestion. However, a return visit to IL Borro just wasn't possible for many reasons, including travel restrictions due to the pandemic. But I definitely wanted to have the vow renewal because I had something pretty special in mind. So, we decided on a nice local restaurant.

Here I want to share an extraordinary experience that happened to me a few months before the ceremony. I was at work in the wine department at Albertsons. Suddenly, I felt this overwhelming river of love for Becky throughout my entire being. It was different from the falling-in-love experience I first had in the library. It was so powerful that I had to walk away so I wouldn't encounter a customer. I couldn't speak, and tears were rolling down my cheeks. One wave after another kept coming. After several minutes, it subsided. When I got home, I shared the experience with Becky. With tears, she said maybe it was a touch of God's love for her being revealed to me.

On the day of the vow renewal party, our intimate gathering of guests included our daughter Jessica and her husband Darrin, our son Jeremy and his fiancé (now wife) Lashai, my boss and his wife, new friends, and wonderful lifetime friends, some of whom had been in the room when Becky proposed. Without Becky's knowledge, I had talked with Salvatore about him and his wife, Tini, joining us via Zoom from inside the IL Borro chapel. He thought it was a great idea. The event began with Becky walking across the room to Andrea Bocelli's recording of "I Can't Help Falling in Love with You." She looked gorgeous in her beautiful dress, and I was a goner.

I recounted the story to everyone how after nine years of dating and no proposal, Becky told me off and then proposed to me over the phone, all in the same day. It had come up several times over the years that Becky felt she missed out on a real proposal by me. Before the vows, I surprised her by getting down on one knee with a diamond ring and proposing to her. Fortunately, she said yes! That, combined with loving vows, brought both laughter and tears of joy to everyone. In her vows, Becky said that after all we had gone through, when we decided to get married, she felt my love for her was real and knew I would be faithful. Salvatore and Tini topped it all off by giving a fabulous, heartfelt toast with their own IL Borro Sparkling Rose, live from Tuscany. The day was magical and full of love. We are so grateful!

I have no doubt that our marriage is a gift. It was a match made in and sent down from Heaven. Becky needed someone to love her and be faithful to her. I needed someone to love and be faithful to. I've asked Becky on several occasions how she knew I would be faithful. She smiles and says, I just knew! That means a lot to me.

When we got the advice to focus on *The Love*, we understood it meant the Gift and the Giver. It is so much more than our sweet feelings for one another. Of course, they are wonderful too.

As the years go by, it has been a joy to learn more and more about what redeeming your bride means. The words redeem and redemption go back to ancient Hebrew roots. It means setting free from captivity or deliverance from bondage. Becky had a lot of hurt and grief. My mission is to love Becky so much that she is healed and set free. I have gladly accepted.

For someone who had been afraid to get married, I feel extremely blessed to have fallen in love with a beautiful woman who not only has a big heart but also a belief in commitment.

~

YOUR MARRIAGE—CURRENT OR FUTURE

Now I am certainly not a marriage counselor. Instead, this is to share what I've learned, and hopefully, help lay the foundation for a beautiful future marriage, help transform problem marriages into happy ones, and help make good ones even better.

Here's the way that I understand marriage was created to work. If the husband gives love to his wife and she receives it, all goes well. The wife becomes radiant, more beautiful, and the glory of her husband, who in turn has a great sense of fulfillment and purpose. Wives who are filled to overflow seem to have more love and respect for their husbands. This is the beginning of uncovering a beautiful mystery. It is so profound that I will leave it to you to discover for yourselves.

Lots of wonderful, unexpected times together will come your way. Even more, the giver and source of love will add many surprises. I got a $1,700 check sent the day before our 10th anniversary. That allowed us to go to Sedona instead of a one-dollar movie. Becky couldn't find her childhood friend that she loved and hadn't seen for decades. I had no idea she was searching for her when I was asked to take an extra table at work and overheard them mention Joplin, Missouri, where Becky once lived. And it was the only time I ever called Becky when I had customers from Joplin. That led to finding her friend and the story that followed. Coincidences? The odds of either of those happening are ridiculous.

Men, your wife should be your glory. How you treat your wife is how you treat yourself. How you think of your wife is how you think of yourself. It is not so hard. Husbands, love your wives. Wives, you should be honored, respected, and adored. These aren't just flowery words. Don't settle for less. If your husband's actions toward you are not coming out of love, don't accept them. That doesn't mean confrontation. It's an inner decision you can make. I am so grateful that my wife doesn't compromise, and she never should. Choose love when differences come up instead of "my way or the highway."

There is a big difference between God's love and romantic, human love. Many people do fall in love and have a wonderful life. Fantastic. We all know that many marriages don't go that way and eventually fall apart. Focusing on allowing God's love to be released can be very healing for your spouse. The rewards can be fun. I've come to understand this better and better over time as I searched for the ways to redeem my bride.

My wife is amazing. When she humbly (and bluntly) opens her heart to point out a shortcoming of mine, the situation usually changes instantly. As soon as I get it, I turn back to the land of the living. The more time that goes by, the less time either of us wants to spend in disagreement. Love is so much more enjoyable.

Allow me first to address the hopefuls for a happy future marriage. So, when is the right time to get married? The answer might sound so simple that you just go ho-hum. Don't let this jewel pass you by. The right time is when the love inside you is greater than your pride.

To those who are struggling, I humbly, gently, and excitedly say to you, it can turn completely around. As a reminder from previous stories, Johnny Baker's marriage was heading toward divorce, and the server from L'Escoffier was separated from his wife, who was living with another man in his house in Mexico. Later, I share another powerful story of a marriage that had the potential to fall apart and had a dramatic change. They all had good outcomes.

Let's try it another way. When it doesn't go the way it was designed, here's what may happen. The man withholds love from his wife. She becomes frustrated, irritable, and unfulfilled. The husband's self-worth begins to go down. As the cycle slowly continues, the wife starts to get into a dominant and aggressive role. The husband feels imprisoned and threatened and responds with some form of anger.

I am describing the classic mother goddess syndrome that goes back thousands of years. Many religions had mother goddesses that they worshipped, like Isis, Ashanti, Ishtar, and Diana of Ephesus. It is pagan mythology and very prevalent throughout the world today. The roles of the husband and wife get reversed, causing growing turmoil and lack of fulfillment in both.

Then come the disagreements, arguments, anger, and way too often, divorce.

Everyone has different trigger points for conflict: money, raising children, lack of support, lack of commitment, and on it goes. If it gets to the point of infidelity, the damage can be significant. Although emotions and feelings may be very intense, none are the truth.

Don't be impressed with either the disagreement or the other person's behavior. That just keeps it going or makes it worse. Be impressed and in awe of the gift of love. It's a choice. Be the one to make that decision and help your spouse through. They will forever be grateful.

The same advice to the young hopefuls may be even more critical in struggling marriages. The overcoming power of God's love has been tried and true for thousands of years. It can take down the walls of hurts, bitterness, resentments, and deceptions that imprison so many people. And when the walls come down, the love can flow like a river.

Hopefully, you know I'm not talking about just settling disputes until the next one comes along. In those cases, the problems still exist. I'm talking about getting rid of the issues to the point that they are laughable. As a reminder, the advice that Becky and I got before our wedding is priceless. If you focus on the love and not each other, all will go well. What a jewel.

She has both small-town Missouri and southern roots. I'm from the Bronx. Need I say more? We might as well have been from two different countries.

Remember:

-You have to want to be happy. It may start with one person. You genuinely have to want a change. Snap out of the fog and recognize that your situation is not unique.

-Keep the fire, romance, and honeymoon going throughout

your life. A good marriage, like a fine wine, should keep getting better.

-Never lose sight that love is the greatest gift in life, and to be able to share it with intimacy is a priceless treasure.

-Differences between two people always exist, and when they are dealt with through the lens of love, it is amazing how small they become and how quickly they are resolved.

-If you remain grateful and humble, it is easy to see that you got the better deal and how fortunate you are.

The VERY GOOD NEWS is that real love does not diminish or dry up. Rather it is meant to grow and be a forever thing. The problem is that people allow all kinds of deceptions to come in, causing them to see through a very tainted lens. It is interesting how many people are aware of some of their limitations and think that when they get married, it will all go away, only to find out the opposite is true. Marriage only intensifies problems; however, **love is greater than all of them.**

There is a better way to get to the heart of the matter (pun intended) to achieve a transformation, rather than just working on the well-established (sometimes successful) methods of resolving conflicts.

The following sign summarizes the choices. Each person in a marriage has to take responsibility for their own decisions. Swallow your pride and choose love. After some time, you'll both discover an extraordinary and wonderful mystery of life.

Caring Love
(Love)
My Way or the Highway
(Pride)

CHAPTER 12

SIBLINGS

BROTHERS CAN RELATE TO SOME DEGREE

For most people, it would be logical to receive a college degree the year of graduation, but that went out the window with my brother and me. In June 2022, Michael called to tell me he was going on a trip to New York to attend a fifty-year reunion of a summer camp where he had been a counselor, as well as to Long Island University/LIU Post, where he had attended. He explained that during his actual graduation ceremony in 1968, with my parents in attendance, he freaked out, ran away, and never got his degree. So, fifty-four years later he arranged with the university to receive his degree in cap and gown.

I couldn't believe what I was hearing and told Michael that, although I finished my courses in 1965, I never attended my graduation ceremony nor got my degree. During that troubled time, I obviously didn't care. Also, being spoiled and having an entitlement attitude, I had no gratitude for my parents who paid for everything.

In 2005, however, my wife suggested it might be a fun idea to get my degree the same year our son Jeremy was graduating from high school. Becky thought it would show the value of completing things, even many years later. That opened my eyes, and I went for it. Although I finished forty years earlier, my degree says 2005, the year it was actually issued. Talk about forty years in the wilderness! And here's what had my brother and me laughing. Both of us opted not to pick up our degrees the year we completed our courses, and neither one of us had a clue about the other's situation.

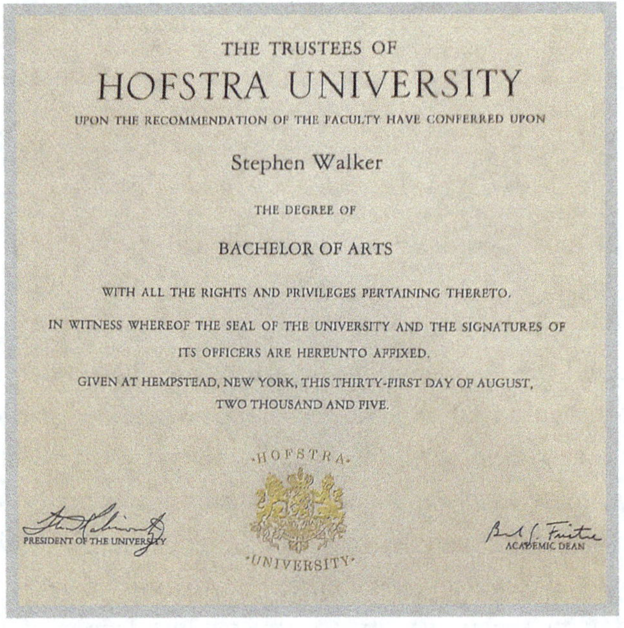

My degree shows 2005 graduation date. Actual year
I finished was 1965.

I greatly appreciate Becky's insight to follow through and complete the process of getting my degree. Up until that time, it never even crossed my mind.

NEED A SIGN?

Strap on your seatbelts for this one (literally and figuratively)! My sister Carol suffered from depression at an early age and was suicidal. I remember my mother telling me that every morning Carol woke up was a great relief to my parents... very tough teenage years.

It got so bad that one New Year's Eve, my parents took her to a hospital where she was put in a strait jacket. While trying to escape from it, she began shouting, "Happy new year! Get me out of this!" They put her in a tighter one and shot her up with Thorazine, a powerful tranquilizer. Then the doctors convinced my parents that Carol needed shock treatments, which were a primitive treatment at the time.

Fast forward around twelve years. Carol came out to visit my brother and me in Los Angeles after our lives had changed. She was prayed for, and something wonderful and dramatic happened. Check out our family photo in the center section, with Carol radiating joy. She got an apartment in Los Angeles and became a successful court stenographer. Her boyfriend at the time, who was a professional photographer, somehow got her to pose for this photo.

Carol with a REAL lion!

Over a period of time, she slowly slipped away from her new life and became somewhat isolated. She was taking an antidepressant yet still functioning on her job. Carol lived in the same apartment for many years. The complex had driveways from the street to behind the buildings where cars were parked. One day she was lying face down on a lounge behind her building, talking to God. As she was telling Him her troubles about believing and needing help, like some kind of sign, she felt this enormous pressure start to come up both her legs. As this overwhelming force moved up her back over her slender frame, Carol was sure she was going to die. A woman driving a Lexus SUV did not see Carol and was running over her. Just as the wheels reached her neck and head, the driver realized what was happening and put the car in reverse, running over Carol's back and legs a second time.

Can you imagine what a horrifying experience that was? When Carol got up with no apparent injuries, it was an incredible shock to both of them! As they spoke, Carol learned the woman was also Jewish, and, would you believe, the license plate on her car read "4 God Pwr." After being twice run over, Carol, who is very thin, was so surprised she was only a little sore.

When Becky and I heard what happened, needless to say, we were shocked! We asked Carol if she would be willing to share her story at Becky's brother's church service the next day. She said yes. We called Gregg, and without telling him what had happened said that he absolutely had to let Carol speak at his service the next day. He agreed.

Gregg had no clue what Carol was going to share and had already prepared his sermon for the day. It was from Psalm 34, and here are a few of the verses: "The Lord is close to the brokenhearted and saves those who are crushed in spirit. The righteous person may have many troubles, but the Lord delivers him from them all; he protects all of his bones, not one of them will be broken" (Psalm 34:18-20). After hearing Carol tell what had happened to her, Gregg couldn't believe how the sermon text he had already selected was so relevant to Carol's story.

The woman who ran Carol over was attending an African American Pentecostal church in downtown Los Angeles. About a week later, Carol and the woman went to the church and shared their story to the resounding cheers of the congregation. I couldn't make this stuff up if I tried, but the story doesn't end there.

One day, Carol went for a hike in the Hollywood Hills, and she parked at an intersection that had non-stop foot traffic. She got back to her car about an hour later and realized she had spaced out and left the trunk open with the keys still in the lock. Add to that, she had left her purse in open view, begging to be taken. NOTHING WAS TOUCHED! Carol thought someone definitely must be looking out for her.

You would think that would be enough, but no. About five years later, Carol went into severe depression and was hospitalized several times. The psychiatrists administered both ECT and TMS shock treatments, as well as prescribing multiple medications, which added several awful side effects. Nothing seemed to be helping, and they kept changing medications.

As her big brother, I was very concerned, especially about all the medications which kept getting added and changed. During that very difficult period, we were visiting our good friends Tim and Linda Pape, and we asked them to pray for Carol. They both had the same discernment: God had Carol in His hand, and He was going to

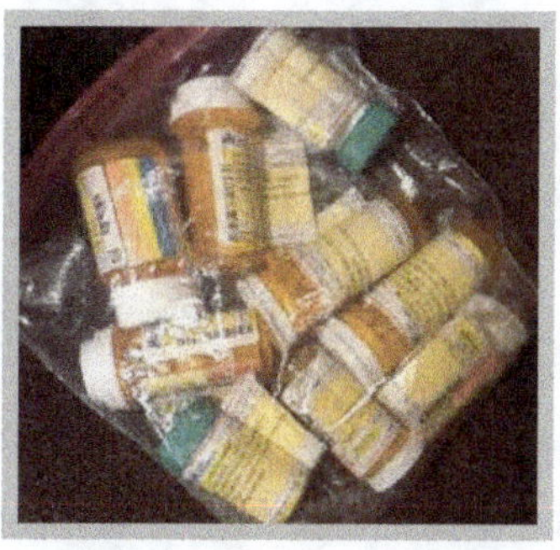

Just some of the meds

work it all out. They told me I needed to let go. That was really hard to do, especially since nothing changed right away. However, I trusted their advice. A few months later, something totally unexpected happened. Somehow Carol learned about a fifty-year reunion Zoom call for the kibbutz she had lived on in Israel. On the call, a man who remembered Carol asked if he could be in touch with her. They began speaking by phone regularly over some time. When Carol went to visit him, my brother and I were shocked. After more than forty years in her LA apartment, and years of sadness and loneliness, she moved across the country and is enjoying a wonderful courtship. She is a very caring and sensitive soul. At age seventy-three, she is now enjoying her life and doing several types of volunteer work, including Meals on Wheels. Michael and I are profoundly thrilled she is happy.

The good news is: It's never too late because God is faithful!

PART FOUR

LIFE—THE WAY

CHAPTER 13

A HELPING HAND?

About a month after my life-changing experience, Doc walked up to me and asked, "What about the Holy Spirit?"

I replied, "What's that?"

He told me it confirms that Jesus is the Messiah, and with it comes additional gifts. I asked if it would get any better than what I was already feeling. He smiled and nodded yes. I excitedly said to come on with it. He prayed for me to receive the gift, and nothing happened.

A few weeks later, my brother and I were back in New York City visiting our parents. While Michael and I were walking down Broadway, something caught me totally off guard. I started to say something, and words came out in a language I didn't recognize. I had heard others speak in what they called tongues, so I asked my brother if I was imitating them. He told me no, and that it was mine. I got so excited that I started running and jumping up and down as people tried to avoid me like another nut case.

The Holy Spirit is a counselor, advocate, and helper. In

everyday life, times arise when we need help in practical situations when we are at a loss of what to do.

WHERE'S THE ARK?

We never intended to be landlords. My wife had wanted to sell our Henderson, Nevada home and move after both kids graduated from high school. She hoped we could relocate to Tennessee and be near our daughter, who would be attending university there. So, we put our house up for sale and, shortly after, received a call from a British TV house hunters' program, *A Place in the Sun*, asking if we would consider including our home as one of their buyer's choices. We were excited about the opportunity, and, a few weeks later, we were told the couple was going to buy our house at a great price. Hooray, off to Tennessee —so we thought.

The bad news was the real estate market in 2008 took such a dramatic plunge that the couple changed their mind about buying in the US. We thought about listing our house for rent, but before we did, I got a call from a couple we knew saying they were aware the house was for sale and asked if we would consider renting. Talk about timing and getting clear direction. They showed up with a check the following morning and signed a two-year lease. We wound up renting a home in beautiful Franklin, Tennessee, just outside Nashville.

A few years later, a new renter moved in two days before his August 1st start date. Early the next morning, I got an urgent message from our tenant's brother. He told me our house was flooded, and the tenant was in the emergency room because of hitting his head racing down the stairs trying to turn off the water. He suggested I call the tenant's girlfriend, who was in from Santa Monica to help with his move. I reached her, and her voice was despondent. She was in the house and explained the flood started upstairs, and she was downstairs, ankle-deep in water, heading to the hospital.

My jaw dropped in disbelief as I tried to grasp what was happening! Minutes later, I got another call. "Hi Stephen, this is your tenant's estranged wife, Carroll, and I'm in your house." I was speechless. The tenant had let us know he was in the middle of a divorce. We had no property manager, and I felt overwhelmed. Here is what immediately flashed through my mind: Is the tenant okay? How seriously was he hurt? Was a lawsuit coming? Will our insurance cover this? Can it be repaired? Who will do the repairs? How long will we be without a renter? Permanently?

Here's what followed. Carroll broke the silence, saying, "Oh, don't worry, I know all about the girlfriend, and I'm here to help with the flood. I have a friend on the way (6:30 a.m. Sunday her time) who specializes in water damage." She sounded so genuine and cheerful. I could not comprehend the unfolding script, and it took a few minutes to adjust to such a hopeful tone. I called my insurance company, and they confirmed we were covered with a $1,000 deductible. Whew! They gave the immediate go-ahead for the emergency water mitigation. Within hours, twenty-six blowers and four de-humidifiers were set up to run continuously for four days.

Fortunately, the tenant recovered from his head injury in a matter of days, and discussions with him were gracious and cordial. After removing the standing water, the insurance company sent an estimator to assess the damages. Then came another call from Carroll saying she knew a good general contractor who would be looking out for our best interest. He and the insurance company worked out an agreement with a final payout of well over $30,000, which was 50% more than an initial offer.

Before work could begin, the contractor told me that the

tenant would need to leave the premises during repairs. That meant him having to put everything in storage and stay in a hotel for six weeks. We were shocked that he agreed. More good news was that Carroll had made sure he had renters' insurance in place before moving in. That covered his hotel cost. The insurance company then let us know they would be willing to pay us the loss of rent. For his goodwill, we offered that benefit back to the tenant. The bottom line was that we got our rent, and he lived rent-free during the time he had to live in a hotel.

To say we were very grateful to our tenant for his extreme understanding in this entire situation is an understatement, as well as to Carroll, who we call our angel. In February 2012, Becky and I went to Henderson for my mom's 90th birthday. While there, we met our tenant for the first time and later went to Carroll's house to meet her. We had such a wonderful time sharing stories.

Here's a summary:

-The estranged wife got a water mitigation specialist while the girlfriend was there. She sent a general contractor who worked with the insurance company to give 50% more. After having moved in only one day earlier, the tenant agreed to put his things in storage and live in a hotel for six weeks.

-Our house got all new paint, carpeting, tiles, and an electric circuit brought up to code.

-One contractor gave us back the $1,000 deductible: the other rebated us $4,000 in cash.

-The upgrades increased the home value. When the tenant moved out, he left us a gift of a removable custom pool fence and garage shelving worth $2,000. It all helped in the future sale of the house.

Anyone could have figured all of this out, right? I have no doubt that help was orchestrated from on high.

A Fantastic Sandwich

Sometimes it's about the basics. It wasn't long after my life-changing experience that I decided to make a permanent move to Los Angeles, got a job, and was very fortunate to find a great apartment at a ridiculously low price. I used all the money I had to move in. When a check I was expecting didn't come in the mail, I wondered where my next meal would come from. My first reaction was that I could ask a friend for something to eat. Instead, to my surprise, I looked up and said, "Okay God, how is this going work out?" About an hour later, the doorbell rang and there stood two of my friends, Michele and Fred, with big smiles on their faces. Of course, my first question was why were they there?

Both of them were part of the same company, Fantastic Sandwiches. They were each driving a different vehicle to deliver food to various customers. At about the same time, they each got a strong urge to stop what they were doing, drive to my apartment and bring me a sandwich. There were no cell phones in those days, and they had no clue whatsoever about my situation. They wound up arriving at the exact same moment. When I shared with them what was going on, we all cracked up laughing. That was the most fantastic sandwich I ever had!

It's Raining Golf Balls!

Sometimes little things in life aren't so little. One Saturday, I drove over to Rancho Park Golf Course in Los Angeles to hit some balls on the driving range. That day both the upper and lower levels were packed. Before I went to buy tokens, I discovered I had left my wallet home—no big deal except for the frustration of an extra 45-minute round-trip.

On my way out, I passed by the ball machine, which was

several feet higher than the sidewalk. At the same time, I looked up toward the sky and mumbled to myself what an idiot I was. Suddenly, I heard this loud clunk and looked to my left. The ball machine broke right at that moment, and a flood of golf balls came rolling right toward me. I couldn't believe it. I immediately found a bucket and filled it with as many balls as needed. A guy who watched the whole scene walked up to me with a big smile and said, "Wow, you have connections!" Talk about a sense of humor, and I don't mean the other golfer or me. It's good to have the right connection.

How wonderful it is that you never have to lose the connection (unless you want to). Over thirty years later, I was having trouble relaxing and living in the moment, always doing something with my mind on the next thing. Can anyone relate? Recognizing that a change was needed, I asked God for help, not knowing how the answer would come, of course. A few days later, I was at a driving range and bought a token for a small bucket of balls. Just before I inserted the token, I looked up and quietly thought that I should have gotten a large bucket instead of a small one so I could spend a little more time enjoying myself and exercising. Instantly, the man standing next to me, who had just bought a large bucket of balls, turned, and said, "These are for you. I have to go." Does it get any more personal and humorous?

The next time at the driving range, I again decided to get only a small bucket of balls. But as I walked toward the ball machine, I looked up and a golf ball was rolling toward me from around thirty feet away. I thought this was wild! When I was about finished, a woman walked up to me and the man hitting balls next to me and said, "Don't let me scare you. This [large] bucket of balls is for you guys." I thanked her and jokingly said that the only thing scary was her kindness. She smiled ear to ear.

Breathing Easy

During my time at Del Frisco's, I got pneumonia, which hit me very hard. I felt delirious. My wife got me over to the nearest clinic. I asked if they took my insurance, and they said they did. After my recovery, I got a hefty bill for services. I made my case that they told me they took my insurance. They said they were required to answer that way but were out of my network and insisted I owed a chunk of money.

It was very frustrating, and going back and forth with them over a few months was to no avail. I didn't want to pay the money. I also didn't want to get a bad credit score. I felt stuck. One evening at Del Frisco's, a customer and I were conversing, and, as I often do, I asked him what his line of work was. He told me that he was head of that very clinic. I didn't hesitate to share my story. Shortly after that, my bill was dismissed. Coincidence?

AFTER THAT INCIDENT, I discussed with Becky the importance of confirming that any doctor or medical service is a provider under our insurance plan. A couple of years later, she called me while I was out of town. Her voice was very shaky, and she started out the conversation, "Don't worry, I'm okay. I got very dizzy yesterday, and it scared me. I went to the emergency room. I'm still here, and they are doing all kinds of tests." Nothing was specifically diagnosed, so she came home the next day with me.

We had good health insurance at the time, and I expected a small bill for the coinsurance. IT WAS A JOLT when I got a $15,000 bill for our portion. Becky knew that she was meant to ask if a doctor or hospital was a provider for our insurance, but she was so out of it upon arrival that she only asked the hospital if they took our insurance. They were not a provider, and there was a huge, unexpected bill. I tried hard to get some resolve, but they wouldn't budge.

Enter Kimberly Roberts, who used to work for the hospital. She was a single mom working two and three jobs to support her daughters. Now the back story. One of her girls sang well but lacked confidence. Kimberly heard Becky was a good voice teacher for young people and wanted her daughter to take lessons. Becky took her on as a student. Not only did her confidence grow, but she blossomed into a beautiful singer. Her mom was grateful. We all became good friends. After considerable effort to reduce the hospital bill, we decided to ask Kimberly if she knew of anything we could do. It wasn't long before the bill did not exist! Love and gratitude can produce unexpected practical rewards when and how you least expect them. Becky had responded to a mother's appeal to help her daughter. She, in turn, was happy to have the opportunity to help Becky.

OPPORTUNITY FOR GRATITUDE

You may recall my prior lung surgery by Dr. Paul Ebert. One evening, over ten years later, there he was, sitting at a table in L'Escoffier with a guest. I didn't recognize him, and "for some reason," his name was mentioned (as sommelier, I wasn't given guest names). I wanted to do everything possible to make sure he had a wonderful time. I recalled to him that I was one of his first few surgery patients at Weill Cornell Medical Center in New York City, and I thanked him so much for the great job.

He dropped his head and said, "When the patient heals well, it tends to make the doctor look good." Talk about humility! While he was looking at the extensive wine list, I asked him what style of wine he preferred. He told me French Red Burgundy (Pinot Noir), a category I love. On our list was a 1972 Le Musigny, an extraordinary wine, priced at $70 before I started working at

L'Escoffier. It would probably be over $1,000 on a restaurant wine list these days. So, let's say it was drastically underpriced. When I suggested that wine, he smiled, looked up, and said that it was precisely the one he was considering, but he thought there must have been a problem because it was priced so low. I assured him it was fine, and he really enjoyed it.

I later learned that Dr. Ebert had become one of the world's top (if not the best) pediatric and adult cardiovascular surgeons and researchers. His extraordinary bio includes being the director of The American College of Surgeons with 82,000 members. I had asked for the best doctor in the hospital and wound up getting the best in the world! Humility is a virtue and a quality of great people.

It was serendipitous that Dr. Ebert wound up in L'Escoffier and that I heard his name mentioned. I am grateful to have had a helping hand even when my life was a total mess, and another one that provided an opportunity to express my gratitude. It's a very personal journey!

Who's Got Your Back?

In the 1980s, I demonstrated and sold Doc's research Pediatric Pulsatile Pump system as a second job. I arranged for a booth at a medical show in Atlanta to demonstrate the system. Before I flew home, I took the equipment on a train and twisted my back when lifting it. I needed help to be able to move due to excruciating pain and went to see a doctor, who, unfortunately, misdiagnosed me. When I returned home, things got even worse. It was so bad that I couldn't work, and all I could do was lay still while Becky maintained her job and took care of everything. I was also very concerned about losing my good sommelier job at L'Escoffier. After many weeks, there wasn't much improvement, but I could walk enough that I wanted to get out of the house. Although I was discouraged, a thought came to go to USC and demonstrate the pump to the chairman of physiology, Dr. John Meehan. That made no sense since I had already seen him, and he was not a potential customer. I decided to go in any case.

I was bent over at a forty-five-degree angle and could hardly walk. As soon as he saw me, he said that I needed to see his friend, Dr. Rene Cailliet, for my back. He sent me his book and told me to mention his name when calling for an appointment, which did get me in much faster.

Dr. Cailliet was head of physical and rehabilitation medicine at Santa Monica Hospital. Becky had to drive me, and she agreed that it was the most unusual exam either of us had experienced. It lasted less than ten minutes with no x-rays, MRIs, or anything of the sort. After a few basic reflex tests with the rubber hammer, he stared intently into my eyes, put his right hand against my left foot, and told me to kick it, which I did. He did the same thing with my right foot, and to my surprise, I couldn't move his hand at all. He immediately got so animated and said, "I've got the problem!" He then explained that swelling on the nerve between my back and my right foot was why there was no feeling or function. He gave me a prescription to take the swelling down and said I should get into bed, not move for three days, and come back. If the medicine worked, great; otherwise, too little too late, and surgery would be required.

When we returned for the checkup, after about one minute, Dr. Cailliet said, "Great, someone else I will never have to see again." I was perplexed because I didn't feel any different from the first visit. With a big smile, he told me the medicine worked, the nerve circuit was open, and all I needed was some physical therapy to get the muscles working again. It was hard to believe, yet it turned out exactly as he said. After a handful of sessions, I was okay and never had a back problem again. And he never billed me! Sometime later, I was told he was top-of-the-world and authored many textbooks.

What made no sense was that, even in painful physical condition, I felt compelled to get out of the house and see someone I knew wasn't a potential customer. It turned out to be exactly the person I needed to see to get well quickly. How good it is to know someone has your back!

Chapter 14

Challenges, Decisions, Outcomes

I n life, troubles come. There's no way around it. Some are beyond control, and others are from bad decisions. Everyone sees life through a combination of beliefs and experiences. We respond through our own lens, and the outcomes can be dramatically different.

Breaking The Cycle

Sometimes we are stuck and continually repeat the same things, not even realizing it. Many problems that we cannot see can be revealed to us so we can be rid of them completely. How can things change if you don't know that you don't know? A story Doc told me made such an impression that I feel compelled to share it. There are enormous implications.

He had a theory that, in some cases, high blood pressure could be caused by people holding on to a deep-seated untruth, building up pressure inside. One of his patients was a woman with chronic high blood pressure, married to her fifth husband. Thinking perhaps a problem existed in the area of men, he came up with a simple experiment to which she agreed. She was asked three questions with a blood pressure cuff on her arm. First, what did she think of her father? She rattled off a long laundry list of bitter complaints. The next question was intentionally on an unrelated topic. The last question was, what did she think of her husband? When she gave identical criticisms about her husband that she said about her father, her blood pressure instantly dropped to normal. Bingo! The doctor, knowing her husband well, told her that he was nothing like that. The light went on, and she realized that she was seeing her husband (and the prior four husbands) through the eyes of bitter resentment she had for her father, which was not the truth. Instead of another probable divorce, she fell in love with her husband for the first time. A year later, she and her husband returned to express their gratitude. They held hands and giggled like two lovebirds. Now that's what a doctor's visit should be.

The story captures a reason for many divorces and unhappy marriages. A husband, wife, or both may, without knowing it, see the other person through the lens of bitterness, resentment, or hurt. This could relate to any situation. Many problems are just deceptions. The sad part is how much happiness and opportunities are missed. "You will know the truth, and the truth will set you free" (John 8:32).

TAKING REFUGE

Safety and protection are primary concerns of human nature. This topic is very meaningful to me, having faced death multiple times. Twice in a rebuilt WWII airplane, we lost all radios in no-visibility storms. If the wind had shifted just a few degrees either time, it could have been all over. If the radios had not come back on by themselves, there likely would have been the same fate. When I got crash instructions and pleaded for my life with God, whom I didn't even know, the clouds parted for the first and only time in two weeks. If you combine all these incidents, I wouldn't be here without protection.

Currently, a war is going on as Russia is invading Ukraine, and the whole world is on edge with uncertain potential escalation. There is increased polarity and division. Violence is erupting in so many different places in unpredictable ways. Crime is on the rise.

Sometimes, it is a little too close to home. Following is an event that happened to our daughter, Jessica, during the writing of this book. On October 25, 2021, Kimberly Morlock, our insurance agent, came over for an annual review of our medical plan. She is professional, personable, and charismatic. We have become friends over the years. Upon arriving, she asked us if we had heard about the shooting incident at the Boise Towne Square Mall a few hours earlier. We had not heard and quickly learned that two people were dead and five others injured, including a police officer. To our knowledge, that was a first in Boise. In the emotion of the moment, I shared with Kimberly something I had been planning to refer to in this chapter. In the Bible, Psalm 91 contains powerful words regarding safety and protection. It was written by King David, who defeated Goliath.

A few hours after Kimberly left, we got a call from our daughter. She said, "I'm okay, but I was in Macy's at the mall when the shooting took place today." Our jaws dropped, and we were in disbelief. She seemed shaken but somewhat calm. Here is the account in her own words a few weeks later:

> *It was the day after my birthday, and I had decided to run over to the mall during my lunch break to look for some boots that I had been wanting. I waited to take my lunch a little later than usual that day. When I*

arrived at the mall, I walked into Macy's and headed for the shoe department, which is in a separate area from the rest of the store on the bottom level. It didn't take me very long to find the kind of boots I was looking for, and I was so happy they were on sale. After I purchased them, I still had lots of time left on my break, so I decided to browse around the store.

I walked to the women's clothing department, still being on the bottom level. After looking for a little bit, I found some sweatpants that were on clearance for a great price. I was ready to check out, so I got in line. I stepped up to the counter, the clerk rang it up, and it was even less than the price tag. Right at that moment, there was a very loud noise. I heard the sound but didn't realize what it was until the store clerk yelled out, 'Those are gunshots! Run!'

I quickly ran behind the counter and ducked down to hide while two other store employees ran over to the storage room that was right next to us and typed in the code. We all raced into that room as fast as we could and slammed the door behind us. Then we dropped down to the ground and hid in the corner. I was in complete and utter shock at that point and just could not believe what was happening. A few minutes later, a lady came running into the storage room from a different entrance in sheer panic. She dropped down to the ground right next to me, put her face in her hands, and then began to weep.

Despite the total shock and fear, I began to pray the blood of Jesus out loud, over and over. I texted my husband to let him know what was going on and asked him to pray also. We hid in the storage room for about forty-five minutes, which felt like an eternity. When the police officer finally came to release us, he asked us to exit the mall and wait outside. The crime scene was like nothing I had seen before in my life. We all had to wait until the mall was fully evacuated before getting to go home, which felt like another eternity. Once we were released, I was so thankful to be leaving in one piece, although still in complete shock.

As I watched the news stories about this tragic incident, I learned that the shooter was just outside Macy's on the mall's upper level when he fired off the first round of shots. The second round was fired inside Macy's near the top of the escalator, and then he ran down to the bottom level and exited the mall, which was right next to the storage room where we were hiding.

My dad told me he was reading Psalm ninety-one earlier that day before he knew what had happened to me. Without a shadow of a doubt, I know that angels were surrounding and protecting me from the moment I got to the mall that day. Where I was standing when the shots went off, next to that storage room, was exactly where I was supposed to be at that moment. God's hand was over me, and I was completely shielded from all danger. In the shadow of His wings, I was safe and took refuge. No weapon was formed against me, and there was no harm that came near me.

Jessica refers to words found in Psalm 91:9-11, "...If you

make the Most High your dwelling… then no harm will befall you… For he will command his angels concerning you to guard you in all your ways…," and Isaiah 54:17, "No weapon formed against you will prevail…" She indeed knew in whom to trust. Jessica prayed the blood of Jesus during an ever-present danger of death. Jesus is referred to as the Lamb of God many times in the Bible. He is also called the Passover Lamb. The blood of Jesus and the blood of the Lamb are interchangeable. These words have incredible power when protection is needed, physical or otherwise.

When I was in Hebrew school at around age twelve, the rabbi read a story about the Jews' exodus from Egypt (~1440 B.C.). I vividly remember having a somewhat mystical experience when I heard the instructions that the Jews were given to smear the blood of an innocent lamb on each doorpost so the angel of death would pass over. A warm feeling went through my body, followed immediately by the thought: As amazing as this story is, there is surely more to it. Many years later, I learned of the most powerful Messianic prophecy written around 700 B.C.: "He was pierced for our transgressions… the punishment that brought us peace was upon him, and by his wounds we are healed… he was led like a lamb to the slaughter" (Isaiah 53:5-7). This was fulfilled around 33 AD.

The ultimate fear of human beings is death. That may not register with younger people, but everyone deals with it sooner or later. I faced it several times in my 20s, which was overwhelming. Many other types of fear cause us to make poor decisions based on the wrong foundation. The good news is that ALL perceived fears are deceptions and can be overcome.

"Perfect love drives out fear, because fear has to do with punishment" (I John 4:18). This means when we allow the door to open inside and that love comes pouring in, it pushes out the fears that are there. It then becomes a choice. Love or fear?

Freedom or bondage? They cannot both occupy the same place inside you.

NEED TO FORGIVE

One of the most significant areas of imprisonment is when you have condemnation, anger, or bitterness toward someone. It is real bondage that often lasts a lifetime. And what about when you offend? Then you're dealing with guilt and self-judgment. In any case, you need to be released and healed. It doesn't matter whether or not you have been truly wronged or hurt. Often the person with the grudge can't see that they contributed to the situation and think it's always the other person's fault. Forget the scorecard and justification. Just know that everyone has to be released.

Forgiveness is vitally important. It has to be honest and from the heart. Once done, it reveals a deep freedom and great mystery. But it can be a very challenging thing to do. Some of the most amazing and miraculous, tear-jerking stories I have ever heard were about people who truly forgave others for doing horrific things. Every time, they said the only way they could do it was with the help of God.

Tim Pape approached me following a small group meeting that I had conducted. He said there was something about me and asked if I would help him through some difficulties he was having. I was honored by his request and mentored him over a period of time. The changes in him were wonderful and encouraging. He has become such a good friend. He shared a personal story that is very relevant to this topic.

Tim had a contentious and distant relationship with his father from his youth into his adult life. His dad had issues, and although Tim desperately wanted to have a close and loving relationship with him, it never happened. When his father died, he feared the hurt and bitterness could never be resolved. One day a pastor mentioned that if you had some strife with a lost loved one, you could sit with an empty chair beside you and speak to them.

The next day, Tim sat down and put an empty chair facing him. He imagined that his father was sitting in front of him and spoke to him, saying he wished things would have been better between them. Sometime later, Tim saw an inspirational movie about a father with his disabled son and the tremendous power of love.

Emotionally moved, he went home, fell asleep, and couldn't stop thinking about the movie when he awoke. It brought him to the point of doing something that he had never imagined. He began to speak to his father again. With a very tender and open heart, he told his father that he forgave him. The dam broke, and he began bawling uncontrollably like a baby. After a good long, healthy cry, he felt a pure and overwhelming love for his dad, something he had longed for his whole life. That freedom and love remain with him to this day. Oh, and he's now happily married to his darling wife, Linda. This story shows that it's never too late to forgive and be set free.

Here's how important forgiveness is. Most people know or know of the Lord's Prayer. Here is a line from that prayer that relates to this topic. "And forgive us our debts, as we also have forgiven our debtors" (Matthew 6:12). In some translations, the word trespasses is used instead of debts.

WHAT JUST HAPPENED?

Judgment is another form of pride that is much too prevalent and is worth a separate discussion. It is wise to judge or discern people or opportunities to make good decisions. It is very destructive to judge or condemn anyone by assuming you have the authority and power over them. The antidote is compassion. If you look at people through this set of eyes, you can help set them free. When responding to others this way, you are accumulating treasures in life. On the other hand, whatever judgments come out of you will come back upon you. I highly recommend plan A.

A story I love shows how a problem can turn into something wonderful and unexpected. When Becky and I lived in Franklin, Tennessee, we attended a small, historic, 200-year-old church. Our dear African American friends, Johnny and Jo Ann Baker, arranged to visit us on a cross-country trip. We were new to the area and didn't know if it was appropriate to invite them to the church. It turned out that the week before, a local family originally from Africa had come to the church service. It went great, and then we knew it would be fine.

So, we took Johnny and Jo Ann with us. After the service, Johnny and I were off to one side talking. Among the attendees were Buzz and Ouida Arledge, a couple who had become our good friends. They were originally from South Carolina. Buzz has deep southern roots and a charming twang. He walked over to where we were standing. Before I had a chance to make an introduction, he looked at Johnny and said, "Hi, I'm Buzz, and I grew up hating black people!" I nearly fell over and held my breath as I turned to see Johnny's reaction. With no hesitation, Johnny replied with a smile, "Hi, I'm Johnny. I grew up hating white people until I met Stephen!" Then they immediately fell into each other's arms with an incredible hug like two long-lost closest friends. We all broke out in laughter. I thought that was the most extraordinary meeting of two strangers I had ever seen!

UNCONDITIONAL LOVE BREAKS DOWN WALLS

Jeremy started having regular anger outbursts at an early age. That really surprised us, and we hoped it would go away in time. But it didn't. As he got a little older, we tried different strategies to overcome the problem. Nothing really worked. There were times he didn't speak to us which may have been his way of controlling the outbursts. It was a very challenging and intense atmosphere for our family.

There was one incident I won't forget. It started out as a little back and forth heated conversation. The next thing I knew was Jeremy literally got into my face, nose to nose. It was a very challenging moment, and admittedly, it shook me. I got upset and raised my voice, which I did not do on other occasions. He turned around and walked into the next room as I stood there troubled by the encounter as well as my reaction.

A moment later, a very clear impression came that I needed to apologize to Jeremy. Are you kidding, why should I apologize? But when the thought persisted, I got it.

I walked into the next room and said, "Jeremy, I need to apologize to you." He looked perplexed and asked for what? I said that the way I responded to him wasn't the right thing to do. As I turned around to walk out, he began to cry and said, "Dad, stop. You don't need to apologize to me, I need to apologize to you." That shocked me! Then he gave me a big hug.

Note: There is a powerful jewel here. If the other person's behavior (child, spouse, parent, friend, etc.) is unacceptable, and you respond in kind by getting upset or angry, then as the saying goes, you are both in a pit. If you take responsibility for your reaction and make a genuine apology without expecting anything in return, at the very least, you will be out of the ditch. In this case a wall came down.

During high school, he got to the point of not wanting to attend school. We felt like we needed to try something different. So we got him out of the house into a one-week program with the local Boys Club. That didn't work, and we kept searching for an answer.

We finally made a painful decision as parents. We enrolled

him in a six-month program in Guadalajara, Mexico. It was run by Americans and included the kids having to do community service as well as completing accredited high school classes. I waited until the day of the flight to tell him, and it wasn't easy getting him to go, but he did. We went to visit him there, and he seemed to enjoy working with the community kids in their outreach program.

After returning home, his attitude was better; however, there were still periods of silence. Christmas was approaching, and my wife came up with the crazy idea of getting him a Burton snowboard, boots, and poles that he had wanted for some time. I protested saying that his behavior didn't warrant any present, let alone the best. He had been giving us the silent treatment for months, and on top of that, I knew it was very unlikely that he would even join us. Moms don't easily give up, and after a few days, she convinced me to do it. She said it wasn't about him not deserving something. It was about giving when he did NOT deserve anything. I reluctantly went to a sporting goods store and came home with items from the bargain rack. Becky immediately asked me if I got the best equipment available, and I admitted that it was just the best price, not quality. She insisted I go back to the store and get the best. I instantly reacted. Then it hit me, and I burst into hysterics. It was about unconditional love, and nothing to do with what was deserved. I was excited going back to the store, and even more so when I came home with the new gift.

Becky's parents, affectionately known to the kids as Grandy and Poppa, were visiting us for Christmas that year. Jeremy has a soft spot for them, and amazingly, his Poppa was able to convince him to come downstairs while we exchanged gifts with one another. Jeremy, as usual, didn't say a word.

After the rest of us exchanged gifts, I told him there was something for him behind the tree. He turned around with a surprised look on his face. It took him a moment to decide whether he was going to even check out the gift. When he peeled off the paper and saw the Burton snowboard, tears rolled down his cheeks, and he spoke his first words to us in some time: "I'm not worthy!"

Although this story speaks volumes, allow me to highlight a few things. This event didn't change everything, but it was a big breakthrough. Growing up, my parents helped me financially, but we NEVER got presents on birthdays or special occasions. I remember on one birthday, just before midnight, I gathered my family to say how hurt I felt that no one even wished me a happy birthday. I say this to point out that giving and receiving gifts was foreign to me. Becky, on the other hand, grew up in a Midwest family where presents were really important. When she suggested to get Jeremy very special gifts, I protested. When she said take back the bargain ones and get the best, I reacted even more. Then it struck me that it took something big, special, and unexpected to change my life. I have learned that something like this can have unexpected rewards in more than one direction!

Parents, Take Heart

When Jeremy came home from Mexico, we learned that he had only completed some of his required high school courses, which put him behind in school. When he realized he wasn't going to graduate at the same time as his friends, it really got to him! Becky and I were encouraged that reality finally struck, and at the same time, we didn't see how it was possible. He would have to complete all his regular school classes, make up the balance of the missing ones in Mexico, and do two additional outside classes all in one year. Jeremy insisted he wanted to do it, so we all met with his principal, who told Jeremy okay, but that he didn't think it was possible. I agreed. When Jeremy walked across the stage with his regular class, the principal ran over to give him a hug, and Becky and I had tears in our eyes. He said when we told him it couldn't be done, that was what motivated him!

After high school and one year of community college, Jeremy attended Boise State University. When he insisted on paying for all his personal expenses by working, we were encouraged. When he chose social work as his major, we were pleased with his desire to help others. It was also great to later hear that he had a job in his field waiting for him when he graduated.

He looked so proud at his graduation. And, of course, we were even more proud. At our hotel room later, in a very somber tone, he said he had something to tell us. My mind had to fight off the worst as I braced the arms of my chair. He said, "You know how parents usually give their children a present for graduation?" He then held up his degree and got emotional as he said, "If it wasn't for your unconditional love and support during my troubled times, I would not be holding this today. So instead of you getting me a present, I am giving you a gift of a cruise to Alaska."

What? In my state of shock, I turned to Becky and asked her if he had just said what I thought he did. We were in tears. I told Jeremy how unbelievably kind and generous that was, but to please forgive me, that I would need a few days to recover. I wasn't kidding.

We had never been on a cruise, and what a great trip it was. One of our port stops was Ketchikan, which is also known as The World's Salmon Fishing Capitol. It had been a very long time since I had been fishing, and the idea of going on a boat with such beautiful scenery seemed like a great thing to do.

In advance of the trip, I booked a charter service. The arrangement was to meet at the dock. We were on time, but nobody showed up. I got a little edgy as the minutes rolled by because this was our shortest port stop. In her loving, sweet tone, Becky said to relax, what's the worry? I tried to call a few times and just got an answering machine. A local tourist official saw me looking around and asked if I had a problem. I explained my dilemma. He told me he knew the boat owner I hired, and he was embarrassed for their tourist reputation and had me follow him.

After making a phone call, somebody was on the way to pick us up. He told us we would have a private boat at no extra charge. That brightened the day. A few hours later, I was back to complaining. No fish were biting. Becky to the rescue. Isn't this wonderful? We're on our own boat, and the scenery is magnificent!

Okay, okay. Then I got a fish on the line, and when I pulled it in, it wasn't a salmon but rather a small baitfish. I grumbled again. It's such a beautiful day says the wife. The boat captain and his assistant were feeling bad and apologetic that we couldn't catch any salmon. Then the captain picked up the tiny baitfish and started waving it around and whistling quite loudly. I thought he might be losing it and felt compelled to ask him what he was doing. He pointed to a tree about half a mile away, saying he was whistling for a bald eagle. I couldn't see anything that far and thought he was joking.

As I kept staring, I saw something flying toward us as the captain said to get our camera ready. We got a video of me tossing my little baitfish to feed a bald eagle that came from half a mile away. The action wasn't over yet. The captain then pointed to a humpback whale in the water nearby, which was bigger than our boat. It looked enormous. Thrilling!

Then as we were getting ready to head back, my fishing rod bent, and I heard *z-z-z-z-z-z*. It was the exciting sound of a good-sized king salmon. To top it all off, the boat owner did not charge us anything for our private charter trip. That was way more than expected and certainly showed that they took customer service seriously. A banner day! Now knowing my wife, she must have prayed. Growing up, my wife was taught: Why worry when you can pray? My upbringing was: Why pray when you can worry? Okay, her way is better than mine.

To me, the most wonderful part of this story by far was the incredible change in Jeremy. In turn, his gratitude and the spirit of his generous gift made the trip so much more enjoyable.

WRONGFUL PRIDE and arrogance can really stir up trouble. It produces a self-righteous attitude that comes with a sense of superiority, as well as looking condescendingly at others. It is actually a cover-up for a sense of low self-worth and is a very divisive and destructive spirit, both to the individual and all others involved. It comes in many areas—religious, social, educational, financial, and more. Sadly, it goes on and on.

The exact opposite is the TRUTH. It can be overcome when you realize how destructive it is and don't want any part of it. Pride and stubbornness are by far the greatest causes of marital problems. It has to be MY way. I know best. Sorry to be so blunt, but if that's the way you think, you DON'T know what is best. How about trading that in for humility? Maybe that's too much happiness and peace? Fortunately for me, all it takes is a look or a few words from my wife at this stage of our marriage. I turn fairly quickly from pride to smiles and hugs. Sometimes I get a piece of duct tape and put it over my mouth. She laughs and recognizes that I got it.

Prideful decisions can have consequences. I got fired from two different outstanding sommelier jobs fourteen years apart for the exact same reason. It is said that the definition of insanity is doing the same thing over and over again, expecting a different outcome. My appeal for time off to attend a medical device show was refused in both instances. I went anyway and was let go. I put my cause above respect for my employer. I deeply regret putting my wonderful boss, Kim Owens (Del Frisco's), in that position. I have shared my remorse with her. And I have apologized to my wife many times. Sadly, it impacted the entire family, especially my wife, who had to pick up the financial load. It's hard to believe I did that.

My restaurant jobs were great. However, I struggled with the idea that I could be and do something with possible greater status, but with the wrong motive. Am I ever grateful for a wife who has stood beside me through those times. The good news is, once I saw it, I could change my mind and go in a different direction. In both situations, I ended up having to get jobs that paid much less and were not as fulfilling. I fell short, and consequences followed.

Sometimes a checklist may help. As a pilot, I knew a checklist was not only essential but required before a flight. And, if you realize you are off course once in flight, you can make a correction and get back on track.

Here is an excellent guideline for making important decisions. Ask yourself what the caring thing is for all involved. It was not loving toward my wife and kids to risk my great jobs. It was not caring and respectful to my bosses to go against the company's request. A very familiar saying is right from the Bible in Matthew 7:12: "So in everything, do to others what you would have them do to you." Can you imagine how many decisions would be different if people followed that guideline?

CHAPTER 15

WHAT'S IT ALL ABOUT?

THE FOUNDATION

THE LOVE

God IS love, and The Love is the gift of God that comes through His spirit, which is different from human love. It never fails. It is kind, always protects, trusts, hopes, and perseveres. It is not self-seeking, nor does it keep a record of wrongs (excerpt from I Corinthians 13). There is nothing more fulfilling, rewarding, or powerful than translating the gift of love into every area of your life.

"Clothe yourselves with compassion, kindness, humility …, and over all these virtues put on love"

— COLOSSIANS 3:12, 14

 'These three remain: faith, hope and love. But the greatest of these is love"

— I CORINTHIANS 13:13

Love is not passive. That was demonstrated in probably the most well-known Bible verse. "For God so loved the world that he gave his one and only Son, that whoever believes in him shall not perish but have eternal life" (John 3:16). This is a direct quote from Jesus. The greatest act of love is laying down one's life for another.

For me, this lesson was revealed in a very unexpected way. Shortly after my life-changing experience and all my illnesses disappeared, I was asked to join someone going to a hospital to honor a prayer request by a family. It turned out there was a man who had a few days to live, and when the host asked me to pray, I ran down the hall saying, "No way, he looks like a ghost." I was convinced to come back and pray. Several days later, the patient was released from the hospital because there was a big change in the X-ray. That shook me so much that I left town for a few days.

Soon after, The Full Gospel Business Men's Fellowship International asked me to go on a touring circuit to pray over people. The thought of going from nine years of despair and ongoing illnesses to praying over people sounded both shocking and exciting! When I mentioned it to Doc, he said, **"You might do better to get grounded in The Love."**

I WASN'T EXPECTING THAT; however I trusted his wisdom, which has proved invaluable. You will see by the end of the book that Doc had a profound knowledge of The Love.

COMPASSION

Jesus said, "All authority in heaven and on earth has been given to me. Therefore go and make disciples of all nations, baptizing them in the name of the Father and of the Son and of the Holy Spirit and teaching them to obey everything I have commanded you" (Mattew 28:18-20).

We all have a good idea of the meaning of authority: a person or organization having the power to give orders, make decisions, etc. Another definition is the power to influence others. Is there another kind of authority? Shortly after my life changed, I was asked to get up in front of our group and use my authority. I didn't know exactly what that meant so I began praying loudly in the spirit. Then I heard, "Keep going," so I prayed even louder. "You're not there yet." I gave it all I had, and the next thing I knew, I had tears coming down my cheeks. I clearly saw in my mind's eye a large crowd beneath a stage with their hands reaching out as if they wanted to be touched by God. Then I heard Doc say, **"Compassion is the highest authority."** What a revelation!

Several miracles in the Bible took place because Jesus was moved by compassion. I believe some stories in this book demonstrate the life-changing power of compassion. To name a few, when I jumped out of the car with concern for the policemen who were holding rifles, they bowed to a higher authority (care for them). When the Ambassador told me that I was crazy for asking for water, I inwardly expressed my concern for our host family. Something dramatic happened that even shocked the Ambassador.

A HIGHER COURT APPEAL

Here is another one where compassion opened the door for a dramatic breakthrough.

One Saturday evening after working on the villa, I decided to go to Norm's Coffee Shop in Santa Monica where my sister Carol and a friend Liz were working. It was 1:30 in the morning, and I was ready for a late-night snack. As soon as I walked in, Liz rushed over to me and told me she was so glad I was there.

She pointed to a young man, who looked to be in his early 20s, sitting at one of the tables. She said that when she approached his table to take his order, he looked very troubled. Liz asked him if he was okay? Both of his hands were on the table face down, and when he slid them apart, Liz saw a napkin with a note he had just written that read, "God help me I'm desperate!" She asked if I would go and talk to him, which I did. We chatted briefly, and he gave me his phone number to follow up.

He shared his story with me on the call. His father had abandoned him at a very early age, which caused him great pain and anger. At age five, he tried to beat his stepfather with a baseball bat. From that point on, he got himself into constant trouble. As soon as he got out of one juvenile detention home, he did something else and wound up back in another one. The pattern didn't stop. At the time of the phone call, he was on trial for robbery. His last time in court, he got angry at the judge, who then told him that there's no hope for repeat offenders like him, and he was going to throw the book at him when he came in for sentencing.

I felt such compassion for his life of non-stop pain and anger. I poured my heart out appealing there was another way, and that he didn't have to go on like this. There was such a wall of bitterness inside, and he didn't want to hear it. He said something to the effect that with the hand he had been dealt, he just deserved to be in prison and suffer.

That really got to me, and I didn't give up. Finally, after some time, the wall broke, and he started bawling like a little baby. He said, "I don't want to go to prison. I can't take this anymore." It was a real breakthrough. In his open state, I asked if I could pray for him and to do two things.

First, would he call the owner of the store he had robbed and apologize to him, regardless of how he responded? I also asked that when he went into court for sentencing, to look at the judge humbly, and not like the father who abandoned him. He agreed. Then I asked God to be with him during sentencing, have mercy on him, and help to heal and change his life. I hoped the sentence would be more reasonable so that when he got out, he would have a fresh new start.

I called him a few weeks later, not expecting an answer. When he picked up the phone, I asked if his sentencing date had been postponed. He told me he had already gone, and that as soon as he walked into the courtroom, without him saying a word, the judge looked at him and said, "Go home. Get out of here!" He confirmed to me that he knew exactly why that happened. I was deeply moved, and he seemed grateful.

Life is in the Giving

The greatest fulfillment comes when you build on the foundation that life is in the giving. It comes from knowing that the greatest rewards and joy come when you encourage, uplift, or impact others. It's a heart thing. When you are rooted in a spirit of giving, opportunities can come unexpectedly. That's how a lot of the stories in this book unfolded. When you are on the path, you have an Advocate and Helper who can make things happen. And just to clarify, I'm not talking here about giving your money or time to worthy causes—that's another topic.

DAILY DECISIONS

It is so simple and yet so hard. The new way is in total conflict with everything we inherited, believe, and have experienced. We are sure it is just how we see it, and we want our own way. Many stories in this book demonstrate how when someone sees what they couldn't see before, there were tremendous changes.

The breakthroughs can come when you are fed up and genuinely want a change. That takes trust and faith; however, the rewards can be incredible and life changing.

Another area that can be challenging is when we get leadings that make no logical sense. When they come from the right place, they always bring about something uplifting and surprising. You may recall one instance where I had an unusual but exciting thought of taking my son to our first Indy 500 race. It was instantly clear that it wasn't my thought, which is why I was having a discussion with myself. It made no sense, so I dismissed it. Fortunately, when it came up a second time, I ran it by Becky, who suggested maybe we should go. It turned out to be such a memorable and fantastic experience for us as well as good timing for our son.

Sometimes we are faced with making challenging decisions. Why not ask yourself, "What is the loving thing to do?" It may change the way you look at things and produce some wonderful outcomes.

THE LIMITS

So, here's a snapshot of the battle. We think we have it all figured out. The Bible says we have ALL gone astray (see Isaiah 53:6). In other words, we've missed the mark. God has offered his side: "For My thoughts are not your thoughts, neither are your ways my ways… As the heavens are higher than the earth, so are my ways higher than your ways and my thoughts than your thoughts" (Isaiah 55:8-9). That doesn't seem even close, does it?

If you want to know the limit to how much treasure we can have from life, just look in the mirror. I hope that got you to smile. It's as simple as that. The more we operate in the old way, the more limits there are to receive the gifts.

The new journey usually begins with great excitement and the sense that everything will be perfect forever. It could and should continue to get better, but all of us have weak spots (some we are unaware of) and are vulnerable to being pulled off track by certain people, circumstances, and causes that seem appealing. When that happens, sometimes very slowly, life seems to get less enjoyable, and like the BB King song, "The Thrill is Gone."

If we put the limits on, we can take them off. The thrill is NOT gone. Whenever you wake up to the reality that you've slipped off the path, you can make a 180-degree turn, and you're immediately back on course. How good is that? It's about making daily decisions. The more we invest in learning about the new way, the more the limits come off.

Don't Stop Until You Know That You Know

You only have one go-round in life. If there is an ANSWER, and a wonderful and amazing one at that, don't you want to find it?

There are currently close to eight billion people in the world. Around 5.4 billion follow, to some degree, the five largest religions. There are many others. Each is very different. Add to that various causes and ideologies, which some people turn into "religions."

It reminds me of the long-running TV game show, *To Tell the*

Truth. For those not familiar with the program, three guests are present. Something true is read about one of the guests, and four panelists ask questions. The real guest must tell the truth, and the impostors lie. It is baffling how often the panelists did not guess the right person. So, what IS the truth?

The truth found me! Although I was forbidden from ever saying the name Jesus, when it came up from inside me, I was overwhelmed with peace and hope, unlike anything I'd ever imagined. All my longtime illnesses, one of which was diagnosed as permanent, instantly disappeared. That was a living, transformative, personalized experience. **I knew that I knew…** and it has gotten even better.

My passionate appeal is that you find the answer for yourself so that you know it is real. How do you get THERE if you don't know where it is? That's the title of this book. Many people are searching but may not be consciously aware of it. Others are working at it. The answer will come if you want it and mean it. Just ask in a way that is real to you. The answer can come in so many ways. God knows exactly how to reach each one of us.

There is a promise that everyone will get "knocks on their door," because God is reaching out to everyone in a very personal way. It DOESN'T matter how good or bad you have been or how unworthy you feel. All that is important is that you receive the gift being offered so you are forgiven, washed clean, set free, and have a wonderful, amazing life to follow!

IS THERE A PURPOSE OR CALLING FOR MY LIFE?

Here is an extraordinary true story I had the privilege of personally hearing. It is about a man who had the limits on his whole life, then took them off. It should cut through all concerns and excuses that you are not worthy, not good enough, or have nothing to offer.

My brother Michael has pastored a church in downtown Denver for thirty years. A little over ten years ago, he was given a gift of the oldest historic Jewish synagogue building in Denver. With generous donations from the community, it was renovated and is now called Church in the City Beth Abraham. On December 3, 2021, there was a combined celebration of the 100th anniversary of the synagogue and thirty years of the church. While Michael was trying to decide who would be the keynote speaker, he received a newspaper article about Floyd Ridley, who had received the Kentucky Colonel Award and was a sought-after speaker. The award is given for noteworthy accomplishments and outstanding service to community, state, and nation. Many notable recipients include Winston Churchill, President Lyndon B. Johnson, President Ronald Reagan, Mohammed Ali, Mario Andretti, and others. Michael hadn't seen Floyd in almost thirty years. He agreed to come, told his story at the event, and has kindly allowed me to share it.

Floyd had a very troubled childhood, and by the age of sixteen, he had chosen a life of living in the streets, doing drugs, drinking, crime, and gang-banging. He was a hobo and lived on trains. His goal was to become king of the annual hobo convention held every August. Before he moved to Denver, he spent six years in the state penitentiary in Western Pennsylvania. After his release, he faced additional serious charges in New York but somehow managed to avoid a second incarceration. One time he broke his ankle jumping off a freight train in Lincoln, Nebraska. In the hospital, a nurse took pity on him and also took a liking to him. She thought if she married him, he might straighten out. She got pregnant, and they had a daughter. Seven months later, his wife realized Floyd couldn't stop drinking and told him he had to go. In Denver, three years later, he had to go to detox due to excessive bleeding. As hard as it is to believe, another nurse took him home. He married her, and she got pregnant.

Floyd was still shooting dope and drinking, so she threw him out before the birth of their son.

Floyd then lived out of a dumpster next to Michael's original church building, an old Safeway storefront. A friend of Michael's took him home to feed him so he wouldn't freeze in the snow. He also took him to the church, where he recalled that my brother and his wife Brenda treated him kindly. Floyd volunteered to do a few odd jobs around the church because he felt guilty and wanted to give something back. He couldn't get why God would mess with him because he was such a bad person, so he eventually left Denver.

It was back to a life of hurting people. He got shot, stabbed, and beaten half to death. One day on skid row in New York, he saw a meat wagon come in loaded with dead bodies. He was told that they would wait until there was a pile of six, put them in cardboard coffins, and take them to be buried. When he heard that, he said no way was that going to happen to him and left.

About nineteen years ago, he was dying under a bridge in Pittsburgh. He was very sick, and a policeman insisted that he go to the hospital. He stayed for one year, had six operations with IVs and breathing tubes, and was down to 100 pounds. He continued to deteriorate and got down to sixty pounds. One day with another hobo sitting next to his bed, the doctor came in and said, "Floyd, you're not going to make it until the morning." The visiting hobo offered to help take up a collection for the funeral.

That evening, Floyd looked up and said:

"Boss, it's me. I'm going to meet you in a little while. I just want to say a few things before I do. I ain't got no excuses. I'm sorry for the way I threw my life away. I'm sorry for the people I hurt. I'm sorry for not being a better father. If you have just a little bit of mercy left, I need it right now. If you see fit to spare me, I'll give whatever life I have left back to you."

Immediately, he saw a mist at the end of his bed and heard a voice say, "Get up. I have a job for you." The next morning, the doctor came in and asked what time Floyd had died. The reply was that he hadn't, and his vitals were stable. They kept him another forty-seven days, certain he would die, but he continued to improve. He got sober for the first time in his life.

Sometime later, he got a call from a treatment center that offered him a job. They also provided him with schooling so he could be trained. He had his own office and desk and worked with others who were downtrodden for some time. Then he went out on his own under the banner of Renegade Ministries. That work got him the coveted Kentucky Colonel Award.

It had been forty years since he had seen his baby daughter, and he had never seen his son. A friend of his tracked down his first wife, who had remarried. Floyd called and left a message with the person who answered to please give his number to his daughter Jennifer. Three weeks later, Floyd was speechless when his daughter called. She was married with three kids. She couldn't handle the thought of a rendezvous, so they began writing and sending each other pictures for two years. Floyd also located his son, told Jennifer about him, and the two of them connected. One day Jennifer said it was finally time to meet, and the families of both his kids and Floyd had an awesome visit together. That evening, his daughter Jennifer and her husband were overwhelmed by the change in Floyd, and he prayed for them. He had a good connection with his son as well.

A few weeks after the visit, Jennifer called, and when Floyd answered, she said, "Hi Dad!" That was the first time those words had ever come out of her mouth. Floyd was overwhelmed with emotion and asked what had happened. She said that during their visit, she fell in love with her father for the first time!

Floyd Ridley (center) with his long-lost family

What can I say after that story except WOW?! He recently published his second book. If there's a plan for Floyd, there's a plan for you. It may differ from what you think, whether you come from a high position or low. Either way, your life can be enriched, fulfilled, and expanded.

CHAPTER 16

THE BIG PICTURE

Israel: Affects on the World Today and the Future

Israel is mentioned in the Bible over two thousand times, more than any other word. A brief overview of the past, present, and future of this nation may be valuable to understanding "The Big Picture."

ORIGIN

- In 1885 B.C., God called Abraham at a time when the world was worshipping many pagan gods and filled with evil practices.
- The Lord said to Abraham (at age 75), "Leave your country…and go to the land I will show you. I will make you a great nation…and all the peoples on earth will be blessed through you" (Genesis 12:2,3).
- The Lord made a covenant with Abram: "To your descendants I give this land {Israel}" (Genesis 15:18).

- God promised that a son through his own body would be the heir, even though his wife Sarah was barren. "Abraham believed the Lord, and it was credited to him as righteousness" (Genesis 15:2-6). That is why Abraham is called "The father of faith."

Note: This changed the world forever, and if that sounds like an overstatement, strap on your seatbelt … it has been and will be an amazing ride.

- Abraham (age 100) – Sarah (age 90) bears a miracle son Isaac. (Genesis 21:1,2)
- Isaac's son Jacob wrestled with an Angel, and God changed his name to Israel, which means one who struggles with God. (Genesis 32:22-28)
- Jacob had twelve sons with four wives, and they became the twelve tribes of Israel.

HISTORY

Exodus: The Passover

The Israelites were enslaved in Egypt. God called Moses to deliver them, and he appealed to Pharoah to let his people go. Pharoah hardened his heart which led to ten plagues, the last of which was the killing of every firstborn in Egypt. God gave Moses instructions to the whole community.

Each man was to slaughter a male lamb without defect. Then they were to put some of the blood on the sides and tops of the doorframes of the houses. "I will strike down every firstborn in Egypt; when I see the blood, I will pass over you" (Exodus 12:3-13). This was a precursor to the Lamb of God (Jesus).

After the last plague, God opened the Red Sea as the Israelites escaped; the Egyptians who followed all died. (Exodus 14:21-29)

God told Moses to tell the house of Jacob: "If you obey me fully and keep my covenant, then out of all the nations you will be my treasured possession. You will be for me a kingdom of priests and a holy nation" (Exodus 19:3-6). This will come to pass in the future in a dramatic way.

THE TEMPLES
Building, Destruction, Rebuilding

David & Solomon

King David was called a man after God's own heart. His son Solomon (the wisest man on earth) was given the decree to build the First Temple, which was completed around 966 B.C. It was destroyed by the Babylonian King Nebuchadnezzar, 587/586 B.C., who then took the Jews into exile for 70 years. (2 Kings 25:8-11) Jeremiah prophesied the exile (Jeremiah 25:11), then gave a wonderful promise: God would come and bring them back saying, "I know the plans I have for you, ... plans to prosper you and not to harm you, plans to give you hope and a future" (Jeremiah 29:10-13).

Cyrus the Great, King of Persia, decreed the rebuilding of the Second Temple in 537 B.C. It was completed in 515 B.C. (Ezra 1:2-4)

PROPHECY
(relating to past, current and future events)

Prophecies are messages from God that confirm His existence, purpose and will. The sixteen books of the Bible referred to as the Prophets are between around 800 B.C. and 400 B.C. Earlier prophecies go back as far as Abraham, Moses, and David (The Psalms), etc. A large number of them have already come to pass, a few are happening today, and some are yet to come. How could all of them have been fulfilled without divine inspiration?

Keep in mind: "1,000 years is as a day with the Lord" (2 Peter 3:8).

Prophecies fall primarily into four major categories: The Jews, the nation of Israel (past, present, future), the Messiah, the Gentiles. Here is a small sample.

JEWS AND ISRAEL

- "It is not because of your righteousness that the Lord your God is giving you this good land (Israel) to possess, for you are a stiff-necked people." Message delivered by Moses around 1445 B.C. (Deuteronomy 9:6)
- "These people (the Jews) have stubborn and rebellious hearts" (Jeremiah 5:23 ~ 600 B.C.).
- "O Jerusalem, Jerusalem, how often have I longed to gather your children…but you were not willing. You will not see me again until you say, 'Blessed is he who comes in the name of the Lord'" (Matthew 23:37-39 ~ 32 A.D.), Jesus lamenting over Jerusalem. He then prophesied that the Temple would be totally destroyed (Matthew 24:2). The Romans destroyed it in 70 A.D.
- "I will gather you back from the nations and bring you back from the countries where you have been scattered, and I will give you back the land of Israel again." (Ezekiel 11:17 ~600 B.C.). It wasn't until 1948 that Israel became a nation again!

MESSIANIC

THERE ARE hundreds of specific prophecies about a Messiah the prophets knew nothing about. Here are a few that are amazing.

Isaiah: Suffering and Purpose

- "He was pierced for our transgressions, he was crushed for our iniquities; the punishment that brought us peace was upon him, and by his wounds we are healed" (Isaiah 53:5).
- "The Spirit of the Lord is on me, because he has anointed me to preach good news to the poor. He has sent me to proclaim freedom for the prisoners and recovery of sight for the blind, to release the oppressed, to proclaim the year of the Lord's favor" (Isaiah 61:1,2).

Jesus quoted this scripture in the Temple in Jerusalem. (Luke 4:18,19)

Note:

Peter Stoner, Chairman of Mathematics, Pasadena City College, calculated the odds of Jesus fulfilling 8 of 300+ prophecies are one in one hundred quadrillion (10 to the 17th).

Daniel: Extraordinary pinpoint accuracy (written ~538 B.C.)

"From the issuing of the decree to restore and rebuild Jerusalem until the Anointed One, the ruler, comes, there will be seven sevens and sixty-two sevens" (Daniel 9:25).

THE ARCHANGEL GABRIEL gave this message and told Daniel that he was "A man highly esteemed."

Commandment to Restore Jerusalem	The 69 Weeks Seven = 7 Years One Year = 360 Days (Babylonian)	The Messiah The King
*Decree of Artaxerxes Longimanus March 14, 445 B.C.	69 X 7 X 360 = 173,880 days 445 B.C. – 32 A.D. = 173,740 days March 14th – April 6th = 24 days Leap Years = 116 Total = 173,880 days!	The Triumphal Entry April 6, 32 A.D,

This chart shows that Jesus made his Triumphal Entry on the <u>EXACT DAY</u> given in the prophecy – It was the ONLY day Jesus allowed the crowds to proclaim Him King!

* The starting point came almost 100 years AFTER the prophecy!

GENTILES

After Paul's dramatic conversion on the Road to Damascus, he became an apostle to the Gentiles. In the 11th chapter of the book of Romans (~ 56 A.D.), he explained that because of the transgression of Israel, salvation has come to the Gentiles to make Israel jealous. He also wrote that all Israel will be saved in the future.

"This mystery is that through the gospel the Gentiles are heirs together with Israel, members together of one body, and sharers together in the promise in Christ Jesus" (Ephesians 3:6).

CURRENT SITUATION: ISRAEL AND THE MIDDLE EAST

ISRAEL BECAME a State on May 14, 1948, after being destroyed in 70 A.D. (1,878 years later).

Against all odds!

They were immediately attacked by five neighboring countries (Lebanon, Syria, Egypt, Iraq, Jordan) and survived.

>1967 - Six-day war: Egypt, Syria, Jordan

>1973 - Yom Kippur war: Egypt and Syria

>2005 - Israel withdraws from Gaza

>October 7th, 2023 – Israel attacked by Hamas from Gaza: Major turning point! Psalm 83 (~3,000 years ago)

"See how your foes rear their heads. With cunning they conspire against your people; they plot against those you cherish. 'Come,' they say, let us destroy them as a nation, so that Israel's name is remembered no more." Sound familiar?

Modern names of the nations in the Psalm: Lebanon, Syria, Iraq, Yemen, Palestine, Gaza

FUTURE WAR: GOG & MAGOG
(PROPHECY ~2,600 YEARS AGO)

Ezekiel gives a very detailed account of a future invasion of Israel by a massive army of nations led by Russia and Iran, including Ethiopia, Turkey, Libya, Syria, Lebanon, Yemen, and Sudan.

When: It will come at a time when the people of Israel are living in safety. The "motive" of the attack will be to plunder silver, gold, livestock, etc. Over the last 15 years there have been significant gas and oil discoveries in Israel. God will do something extraordinary, which will show Him holy in the sight of many nations. (Ezekiel 38, 39) – ALL the invading nations will turn and kill each other! It will take Israel seven months to bury the bodies.

Notes:

- Israel did not exist for 1,878 years.
- Russia and Iran have been enemies for a long time UNTIL recently.

THE THIRD TEMPLE

◆ Many prophecies and scriptures in both the Old and New Testament make it clear that a third temple must be rebuilt before the return of the Messiah, who will sit on David's throne.

◆ The Temple Institute was established for that purpose in 1987, with headquarters in the Jewish Quarter of the Old City in Jerusalem. Architectural plans are already in place, and they have built several sacred vessels which are ready to go in the temple.

YouTube: The Third Holy Temple Plans Have Begun – The Temple Institute

◆ There will be a return to animal sacrifices. As in the times of the Torah given to Moses (first five books of the Old Testament), a red heifer without blemish was required by the priests for the purification of sin. Recently, five red heifers were shipped from Texas to Israel. They have been approved by rabbis as a potential to find the perfect one!

It is getting closer …

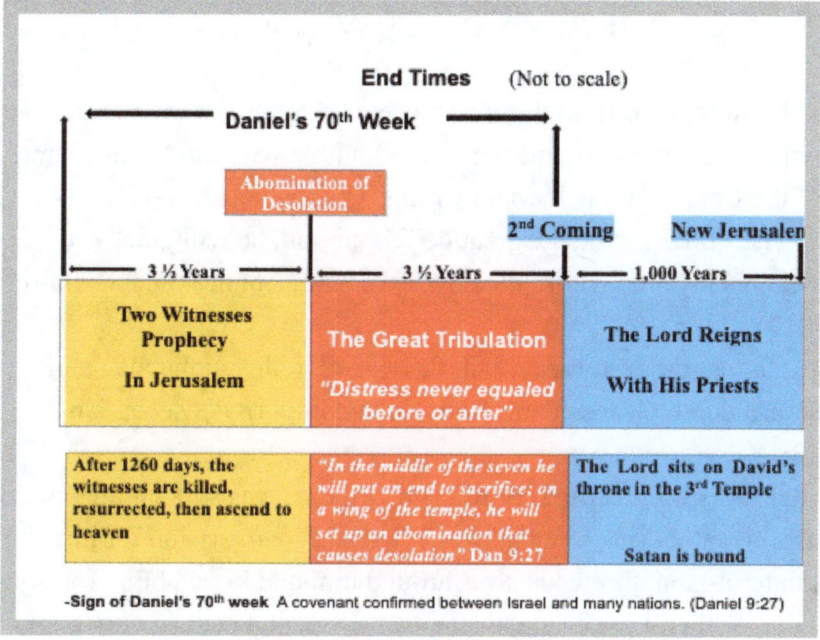

-Abomination that causes desolation: The antichrist erects a large statue of himself in The Holy of Holies in the Temple.

JERUSALEM/ISRAEL: END TIMES

> "On that day, when all the nations of the Earth are gathered against her, I will make Jerusalem an immovable rock for all the nations"

— ZECHARIAH 12:3

> "In the whole land two-thirds will be struck down and perish"

— ZECHARIAH 13:8

THE REMNANT: SURVIVING JEWS

- "I will remove from this city those who rejoice in their pride…I
will leave within you the meek and humble who trust in the name
of the Lord. They will do no wrong" (Zephaniah 3:11-13).
- "The Lord… will take great delight in you, he will quiet you
with his love, he will rejoice over you with singing" (Zephaniah
3:17).
- "On that day, a fountain will be opened to the…inhabitants of
Jerusalem to cleanse them from sin and impurity" (Zechariah
13:1).
- **Israel is the Prodigal Son!** "But while he was still a long way
off, his father saw him and was filled with compassion for him; he
ran to his son, threw his arms around him and kissed him. The son
said, 'Father, I have sinned against heaven and against you. I am
no longer worthy to be called your son.' The father said… Let's
have a feast and celebrate. For this son of mine was dead and is
alive again; he was lost and is found" (Luke 15:20-24).

JESUS SPOKE this parable about Israel which reveals the heart of
The Father.

THE LORD COMES AND REIGNS

- "I will pour out on the house of David and the inhabitants of
Jerusalem a spirit of grace and supplication. They will look on
me, the one they have pierced, and mourn for him as one mourns
for an only child" (Zechariah 12:10).
- "I will gather all the nations to Jerusalem to fight against it.
Then the Lord will go out and fight against those nations. On that
day his feet will stand on the Mount of Olives,…and it will be
split in two. Then the Lord my God will come and all the holy

ones with him. The Lord will be king over the whole earth"
(Zechariah 14:2, 3, 4, 5, 9).

"IN THAT DAY"
(a prophetic expression referring to the end times)

- Egypt and Syria: "There will be a highway from Egypt to
Assyria. The Assyrians will go to Egypt and the Egyptians to
Assyria. The Egyptians and Assyrians will worship together. In
that day Israel will be the third, along with Egypt and Assyria, a
blessing on the earth. <u>The Lord Almighty will bless them, saying,
'Blessed be Egypt my people, Assyria my handiwork, and **Israel
my inheritance'" (Isaiah 19:23-25).**</u>
- Iran: "I will set my throne {spiritual} in Elam {Iran} and destroy
her king and officials, declares the Lord" (Jeremiah 49:38).
- Then the survivors from all the nations that have attacked
Jerusalem will go up year after year to worship the King, the Lord
Almighty, and celebrate The Feast of Tabernacles" (Zechariah
14:16).

There will still be people around the world who do not yet
believe in God. The Jews (remnant) will be saved "by fire." They
will be the most humble people on the face of the earth. The
Jewish nation will at last be a holy nation, a kingdom of priests, as
promised in Exodus 19:3-6, 3,400+ years ago. Just imagine, the
people of the world who come to Jerusalem may tell the Jews that
they are afraid to face the Lord because they have been rebellious.
The Jews can tell them, *We were TWICE as rebellious, and He
STILL SAVED US!*

Do You See What I See?

Here's a 'warm-up' to the Grand Finale.

In January of 1974, I met Dick and Marge Olson, along with their two children, Kim and Mark. Dick and Marge almost always had big smiles and were very encouraging to me. Dicko, as everyone called him, looked a lot like Sonny Bono (Sonny & Cher) and was often mistaken for him. He loved to joke around and had a contagious sense of humor. My brother Michael and I loved trying to outdo him with our one-liners. From 1976 until Dicko's stroke in 1993, Dick and Marge toured with top musical groups, including: Earth, Wind & Fire; The Emotions; Denice Williams; Ricky Lee Jones; John Denver; Shirley MacLaine; Kenny G; and Donna Summers. Dicko was either driving the equipment truck or stage managing, and Marge was doing wardrobe. Along the way, they moved to Todos Santos, a charming town on the Baja peninsula, about an hour north of Cabo San Lucas. Whenever they weren't touring, they would be in Mexico running their business, as well as working with rehab centers and starting a children's home.

In the summer of 2014, Dicko went to Loveland, Colorado by himself to be with his son Mark and wife Dana, for treatment of pancreatic cancer that had spread to his hip, and ultimately to the liver. When Kim called me to say he was in hospice on short time, I jumped a plane to Denver the next morning and drove there with my brother Michael. Upon arriving, we learned that Dicko was heavily medicated for pain and virtually unresponsive for at least twenty-four hours. The hospice nurse said he could go at any moment. I told him that I loved him. Then a wild thought came to me. I asked Michael to stand with me next to Dicko and spoke to him as if he could hear. "Dicko, it's Stephen and Michael here. The two of us Jewish brothers have a plan to get your money when you're gone." He then instantly bolted up into a sitting position with his mischievous smile and said, "No way that is going to happen!" We burst out laughing.

Dicko

Shortly after that, he struggled with his words to get a powerful message across to all the family and friends who were gathered around him that day. He said that he had seen Jesus and made a passionate plea: "It's real! You've got to take it seriously. It's close, so close." He was excited about where he was going, and a few days later, on November 6, 2014, off he went.

I learned about a couple of other interesting events in Dicko's last days. Every so often he would wake up with his eyes wide open in a bold stare and then slowly and intentionally move his head around the room. There seemed little doubt he was seeing something. Also, from time to time, without waking up, he would raise his hand up and break out into a big smile. The assumption was it was a relief from his pain, until a nurse shed a little different light on what that meant. She told Kim that her own father had gone through almost the identical illness a few years earlier, and that before he passed away, he would also lift his hand and smile. On one of those occasions, the nurse asked her dad what he was doing. He bolted awake and said, "I'm reaching into Heaven!"

THE GRAND FINALE! HEAVEN

I've saved the best for last because it can be the next step of the journey. I had my first clue about the reality of Heaven around age five. It was a tiny glimpse, yet it seemed so exciting that I was willing to trade my life down here to join the party up there. All I knew was that I wanted to be there because they were running around having so much fun!

I've been most fortunate and privileged to have personally been in contact with three people who shared their experiences of being taken up to Heaven. They all said they heard the most beautiful, exhilarating, and indescribable music, unlike anything on earth. I've also read several other books in which very account had a similar incredible theme.

After Jesus reigns for 1,000 years, here is what follows:

"Then I saw a new heaven and a new earth…I saw the Holy City, the new Jerusalem, coming down out of heaven… Now the dwelling of God is with men, and he will live with them…He will wipe away every tear from their eyes. There will be no more death or mourning or crying or pain" (Rev 21:1-4).

"The glory of God gives it light, and the lamb is its lamp" (Rev 21:23).

It was through Doc that my life changed. He was a retired heart surgeon and cardiologist honored in Life Magazine for his primary work on the Artificial Heart. He was trained in eight universities. How could someone of that stature take time for someone like me? Why? Several years after we met, he shared his extraordinary vision. He wrote that he considered himself of some value up until that moment, and afterward, he felt like a speck of dust that had just been expanded.

HE SUMMED up what he saw and experienced with these words:

"Awesome Love! Overwhelming, Ecstatic, Unending Love!
The Light. The Glory. The Majesty. The Purity. The
Awesome Power. The Ecstatic Joy. The overflowing
dynamic refreshing energy of Peace!
GOD IS WONDERFUL!"

~

SO, DO YOU WANT TO JOIN THE PARTY?

NOTES

7. Job Challenges or Opportunities?

1. *"Waiting tables may be the most stressful job of all, researchers say."* Amy Reiter, Food Network
2. Statista.com

ACKNOWLEDGMENTS

My brother Michael's life dramatically changed for the better, and even though we were at odds for twenty-eight years, he wanted the same for me. He extended an invitation to visit him and meet his new friends, and that allowed my unexpected, life-changing experience. I'm so grateful to him.

Marilyn Berger was not only a very good friend but a shining light. Her example was of great value to me.

Several people passionately encouraged me to write my story: Chuck Flynn was a highly respected, international minister for many years. He said he had never heard anything like my story, and it should go out to others. Tracy Suiter, whom I had never met, approached me at a meeting and delivered a powerful, unsolicited message: "Write, write, and the outcome will help you fulfill your purpose." I thank Vicki Mundy, who had a compelling discernment that I should write a book. She had no idea I already started one. Heartfelt thanks to Gary Gilmore, who continually urged me to complete this book. He is very missed. And to the many others who gave encouraging feedback along the way, a big thank you!

I deeply appreciate the friends and family who allowed me to share their stories with the hope of encouraging others: Buzz Arledge, Johnny Baker, Carroll Beeson, Polly Greer, Tim Pape, Floyd Ridley, Kim Rinker, Kimberly Roberts, Bob Vernon (father-in-law), Gregg Vernon (brother-in-law), Carol Walker (sister). Thank you to our daughter Jessica and our son Jeremy.

For all the others whose stories are in the book, it was wonderful to share those experiences with you.

Writing a book doesn't happen without the heart and talent of a team that gets into the nitty-gritty. Many thanks to Judy Gilmore for getting this project on a solid foundation, as well as her technical support and inspiring the creative cover design. (gilmoregraphics@sB.C.global.net) I greatly appreciate Stacey Smekofske for invaluable publishing coaching, final proofing and formatting, getting this to the finish line, and adding her input to the cover design. (stacey@editsbystacey.com) When your wife is the initial typist and editor, be assured there are no shortcuts or compromises. Becky held me to a high-quality standard, which she does in every area of my life. She is amazing!

Good friends, too many to list, are among life's greatest treasures. To be able to laugh and cry together (in some cases for more than forty years) is very special. Thank you all for sharing the ongoing journey.

To the One who rescued me from death many times, and, more importantly, rescued me from myself, thank you God!

About the Author

After growing up in New York City and Long Island, Stephen has lived and worked in the Los Angeles and Mammoth Lakes, California areas, Phoenix, Las Vegas, and Franklin, Tennessee. He currently resides in Boise, Idaho, with the love of his life, Becky, and their mischievous maltipoo, Chanté. After nine years of dating, Becky told him to "go jump in a lake," then proposed to him. On  their 35th anniversary and vow renewal, he finally proposed to her, ring and all. Now he sometimes introduces himself as Mr. Becky. Reality at last!

Stephen enjoys traveling and speaking other languages. He still has big dreams; his family sometimes calls him Walter Mitty, like the daydreamer in the book and movie.

His greatest joy and fulfillment come when he can give hope, direction, encouragement, mentor, share stories, and make people laugh. That passion has produced many surprising stories with unexpected rewards. Career recognitions and accomplishments include: Sommelier-of-the-Year, California Restaurant Writers Association; feature article in LA Magazine, "Eight Great Jobs"; #1 in the US, sales/sales management, Nest Entertainment.

"Stephen is a role model with unsurpassed hospitality skills."

-Larry Smith, GM, Chaparral Restaurant, Camelback Inn,
(Then a 5-Star Marriott), Scottsdale, Arizona

Learn More at WhereIsThere.org

www.ingramcontent.com/pod-product-compliance
Lightning Source LLC
Chambersburg PA
CBHW051518150726

47997CB00001B/301